THE CHINESE

COMING TO AMERICA

THE CHINESE

C.J. Shane, *Book Editor*

Bruce Glassman, *Vice President*
Bonnie Szumski, *Publisher*
Helen Cothran, *Managing Editor*
Laura K. Egendorf, *Series Editor*

GREENHAVEN PRESS
An imprint of Thomson Gale, a part of The Thomson Corporation

THOMSON
GALE

Detroit • New York • San Francisco • San Diego • New Haven, Conn.
Waterville, Maine • London • Munich

For more information, contact
Greenhaven Press
27500 Drake Rd.
Farmington Hills, MI 48331-3535
Or you can visit our Internet site at http://www.gale.com

Cover credit: © Robert Holmes/CORBIS
Library of Congress, 24, 99

LIBRARY OF CONGRESS CATALOGING-IN-PUBLICATION DATA

The Chinese / C.J. Shane, book editor.
   p. cm. — (Coming to America)
Includes bibliographical references and index.
ISBN 0-7377-2150-2 (lib. bdg. : alk. paper) —
   1. Chinese Americans—History. 2. Chinese Americans—Biography.
3. Immigrants—United States—History. 4. Immigrants—United States—
Biography. I. Shane, C.J. II. Coming to America (San Diego, Calif.)
E184.C5C4745 2005
973'.04951—dc22   2003067533

Printed in the United States of America

CONTENTS

Chapter 2: Early Struggles and Achievements from the First Wave to World War II

Chapter 4: Portraits of Chinese Americans

FOREWORD

In her popular novels, such as *The Joy Luck Club* and *The Bonesetter's Daughter*, Chinese American author Amy Tan explores the complicated cultural and social differences between Chinese-born mothers and their American-born daughters. For example, the mothers eat foods and hold religious beliefs that their daughters either abhor or abstain from, while the daughters pursue educational and career opportunities that were not available to the previous generation. Generation gaps occur in almost all families, but as Tan's writings show, such differences are even more pronounced when parents grow up in a different country. When immigrants come to the United States, their initial goal is often to start a new life that is an improvement from the life they experienced in their homeland. However, while these newcomers may intend to fully adapt to American culture, they inevitably bring native customs with them. Immigrants have helped make America broader culturally by introducing new religions, languages, foods, and different ways of looking at the world. Their children and subsequent generations, however, often seek to cast aside these traditions and instead more fully absorb mainstream American mores.

As Tan's writings suggest, the dissimilarities between immigrants and their children are manifested in several ways. Adults who come to the United States and do not learn English turn to their children, educated in the American school system, to serve as interpreters and translators. Children, seeing what their American-born schoolmates eat, reject the foods of their native land. Religion is another area where the generation gap is particularly pronounced. For example, the liturgy of Syrian Christian services had to be translated into English when most young Syrian Americans no longer knew how to speak Syriac. Numerous Jews, freed from the European ghettos they had lived in, wished to assimilate more fully into the surrounding culture and began to loosen the traditional dietary and ritual requirements under which they had grown up. Reformed Judaism, which began in Germany, thus found a strong foothold among young Jews born in America.

However, no generational experiences have been as significant as that between immigrant mothers and their daughters. Living in the United States has afforded girls and young women opportunities they likely would not have had in their homelands. The daughters of immigrants, in some cases, live entirely different lives than their mothers did in their native nations. Where an Arab mother may have only received a limited education, her American-raised daughter enjoys a full course of American public schooling, often continuing on to college and careers. A woman raised in India might have been placed in an arranged marriage, while her daughter will have the opportunity to date and choose a husband. Admittedly, not all families have been willing to give their daughters all these new freedoms, but these American-born girls are frequently more willing to declare their wishes.

The generation gap is only one aspect of the immigrant experience in the United States. Understanding immigrants' unique and shared experiences and their contributions to American life is an interesting way to study the many people who make up the American citizenry. Greenhaven Press's Coming to America series helps readers learn why more people have moved to the United States than to any other nation. Selections on the lives of immigrants once they have reached America, from their struggles to find employment to their experiences with discrimination and prejudice, help give students insights into stereotypes and cultural mores that continue to this day. Finally, profiles of prominent immigrants help the reader become aware of the many achievements of these people in fields ranging from science to politics to sports.

Each volume in the Coming to America series takes an extensive look into a particular immigrant population. The carefully selected primary and secondary sources provide both historical perspectives and firsthand insights into the immigrant experience. Combined with an in-depth introduction and a comprehensive chronology and bibliography, every book in the series is a valuable addition to the study of American history. With immigrants comprising nearly 12 percent of the U.S. population, and their children and grandchildren constantly adding to the population, the immigrant experience continues to evolve. Coming to America is consequently a beneficial tool for not only understanding America's past but also its future.

INTRODUCTION

For many years Chinese immigrants to the United States faced pervasive discrimination that restricted most aspects of their lives in America. They struggled against racially discriminatory laws and racially motivated persecution and violence. Despite these persistent obstacles, Chinese immigrants and their American-born children made good use of the American judicial and legislative systems to press their case for equal rights as guaranteed by the U.S. Constitution. Their efforts to gain equality as an immigrant group resulted in a significant advancement of civil rights for all Americans.

Social commentators in nineteenth-century America often claimed that Chinese immigrants were not interested in U.S. culture and institutions, including the law. Many people believed that the Chinese could not be assimilated into American life. San Francisco's leading newspaper at that time, *Alta California*, stated in 1869 that the average Chinese immigrant "knows and cares nothing more of the laws of the people among whom he lives than will suffice to keep him out of trouble and enable him to drive a thrifty trade."[1]

These assertions were far from the truth. Despite the fact that they had come from a society with a political system quite unlike America's system, Chinese immigrants in America were quick to perceive that they could use the U.S. courts to fight discriminatory legislation and to seek equal protection under the law. As early as 1860, Chinese immigrants hired a lobbyist to represent their interests in the legislature of California, the state where most Chinese immigrants resided. In California and other states, Chinese immigrants filed hundreds of lawsuits, often hiring top law firms to represent them. Legal redress was sought both by individuals and by organized groups of Chinese residents, such as benevolent self-help associations and occupational guilds. The Chinese were especially active in the courts during the last four decades of the nineteenth century. The Chinese did not win all their lawsuits, but they did win many that were important to civil rights.

Three types of legal cases initiated by the Chinese stand out as being particularly important to the development of American civil rights law: cases arguing against discriminatory legislation, cases arguing for immigration and citizenship rights, and cases arguing for equal access to public education.

Fighting Discriminatory Laws

Discriminatory laws were passed against the Chinese at every level of government: city, state, and federal. The city of San Francisco, for example, persecuted the Chinese with petty laws meant to punish and harass them as a group and to encourage their departure from the city. State laws, especially in California, were enacted that restricted Chinese residents from owning land, testifying in court on their own behalf, entering certain occupations, living anywhere they wished, or marrying white persons. On the national level, prejudicial laws against the Chinese culminated in the federal Chinese Exclusion Act, which legally prevented immigration of most Chinese to the United States from 1882 to 1943. The Chinese have been the only race or nationality to be denied entry into the United States as a group.

From the earliest days, individual Chinese immigrants and benevolent self-help associations responded by initiating legal action seeking relief from these discriminatory city, state, and federal laws. Attorneys arguing for their Chinese clients based their legal arguments on the U.S. Constitution, the Civil Rights Law of 1870, and the Burlingame Treaty of 1868 between the United States and China, which guaranteed Chinese residents basic rights while residing in America. When Chinese immigrants and Chinese Americans successfully challenged the discriminatory laws, civil rights law was advanced.

An early example of a challenge to a discriminatory city law was the case of Ho Ah Kow. The board of supervisors in San Francisco passed a "cubic air law" in 1870 that required each adult resident to live in at least five hundred cubic feet of air space—a law designed to punish the Chinese, most of whom were racially segregated in the city's Chinatown district, where they lived in crowded tenements. When Chinese residents were arrested and jailed for breaking the cubic air law (in a jail that itself broke the cubic air law), they were subjected to the Queue Ordinance of 1876, which required the sheriff to cut off each Chinese man's queue (long hair braid). The queue was important to the Chinese because a man who returned to China without it was branded a criminal or a rebel.

Ho Ah Kow, a resident of Chinatown, had his queue chopped off when he was jailed for violating the cubic air law. Backed by a self-help group called the Chinese Six Companies, Ho sued. In *Ho Ah Kow v. Nunan*, U.S. Ninth Circuit Court judges agreed with Ho that his civil rights had been violated. The queue ordinance was overturned, and Ho was awarded $10,000 for the "mental anguish" he had suffered.

The decision in *Ho Ah Kow v. Nunan* is significant to civil rights law because it was the first time that the Fourteenth Amendment was applied to noncitizens. The case also affirmed that the motivation behind a law could come under review. In his opinion, Judge Stephen Field wrote,

When we take our seats on the bench we are not struck with blindness, and forbidden to know as judges what we see as men; and where an ordinance, though general in its terms, only operates upon a special race . . . it being universally understood that it is to be enforced only against that race . . . we may justly conclude that it was the intention . . . that it should have such operation, and treat it accordingly.[2]

The Case of Yick Wo

Determined to discourage the Chinese from putting down roots in the city, the San Francisco Board of Supervisors next went after Chinese laundries. Between 1873 and 1884, the board passed fourteen "laundry ordinances" designed to put the laundries out of business. From the *Ho Ah Kow* case, board members had learned to avoid writing laws that openly discriminated against the Chinese because clearly discriminatory laws were vulnerable to being overturned by federal courts. Instead, board members wrote the laundry ordinances to apply to *all* of San Francisco's 320 laundries, not just the 240 owned by Chinese residents. The new laundry ordinances required all laundries to apply for licenses. However, the ordinances were so loosely written that the grounds upon which a license was granted were ambiguous and unclear, leading to unfair application of the new licensing law. All Caucasian-owned laundries except one received licenses, while none of the Chinese-owned laundries was granted a license.

The most important challenge to the laundry ordinances came in *Yick Wo v. Hopkins*. The Yick Wo laundry had been in business in the same location for twenty-two years. The Chinese owner had complied with all city health and safety regulations and had received a certificate from the city health department officer stating that sanitation and health standards had been met. Yet under the new ordinance, Yick Wo was denied a license to operate. Yick Wo, backed by a Chinese laundryman's guild called Tung Hing Tong, went to court to challenge the discriminatory laundry ordinance. The guild hired an eminent San Francisco trial attorney, Hall McAllister, to represent them. The case was initially rejected by state courts, but Yick Wo eventually appealed to the U.S. Supreme Court and won.

The Court ruled, "Though the law itself be fair on its face and impartial in appearance, yet, if it is applied and administered by public authority with an evil eye and an unequal hand, so as practically to make unjust and illegal discriminations between persons in similar circumstances, material to their rights, the denial of equal justice is still within the prohibition of the Constitution."[3]

In *Yick Wo*, the Court reaffirmed the principles set down earlier in *Ho Ah Kow:* The equal protection clause of the Fourteenth Amendment applied to all U.S. residents and the law could be evaluated beyond its words to consider its purposes. The *Yick Wo* decision went even further. According to historians Charles J. McClain and Laurene Wu McClain, "Courts could look at how a law was actually administered to determine whether it came up to constitutional standards. *Yick Wo* took the Court an important step further in its interpretation of the equal protection clause, and the case has ever since been one of the most cited decisions in discussions of that clause of the Constitution."[4]

Seeking Citizenship and Immigration Rights

The fight against discriminatory laws such as the laundry ordinances was only one challenge facing Chinese residents in America. Another challenge was the effort to clarify the citizenship status of ethnic Chinese born in America.

This challenge was taken up by Wong Kim Ark, who was born in 1873 in San Francisco to Chinese immigrant parents. In 1890 Wong's parents decided to return to China, and Wong accompanied them on their trip. He returned to the United States later that year and was readmitted into the United States as an American citizen. A few years later, in 1895, Wong again traveled to China. When he tried to return to his native land, he was denied entry on the grounds that he was not a citizen and was ineligible for immigration under the 1882 Chinese Exclusion Act.

Wong was placed under the custody of a U.S. marshal and detained on his steamship in San Francisco Harbor. Wong hired an attorney, Thomas Riordan, who stated in court that Wong was being unlawfully confined and that his rights as a U.S. citizen under the Fourteenth Amendment were being violated. According to historian Erika Lee, U.S. district attorney Henry S. Foote argued In *Wong Kim Ark v. United States* that "birth within the United States did not necessarily confer the right of citizenship, especially in the case of Chinese, who were unassimilable and unfit for citizenship."[5]

The U.S. District Court for the Northern District of California rejected Foote's arguments. The court's 1896 decision was based upon the Fourteenth Amendment to the Constitution, which begins with these words: "All persons born or naturalized in the United States, and subject to the jurisdiction thereof, are citizens of the United States."[6] Judge William Morrow wrote, "It is enough that he [Wong] is born here whatever the status of his parents. No citizen can be excluded from this country except in punishment for a crime. The petitioner must be allowed to land, and it is so ordered."[7] Wong Kim Ark was released from custody, and he returned to his home.

Foote appealed to the U.S. Supreme Court, but in 1898, the Court let stand the district court's ruling in favor of Wong. In so doing, the Supreme Court rejected race as the determiner of American citizenship. According to historian Iris Chang, America's high court embraced "the judicial principle of *jus soli* ('law of the soil') whereby a person obtained citizenship simply by virtue of being born in America."[8]

Immigration Rights and Chinese Families

The *Wong* decision established citizenship rights for anyone born on American soil after 1898. However, the Chinese continued to chafe under the 1882 Chinese Exclusion Act, as it severely curtailed Chinese immigration. All efforts by Chinese residents to overturn the Exclusion Act failed in the courts. Yet both Chinese immigrants and Chinese Americans continued to challenge these restrictive immigration laws. In their efforts to establish normal family life, they put special attention on the right to bring Chinese-born wives and children to America. Again, the result was an enhancement of civil rights law.

Chinese women were few in number for the first one hundred years of Chinese immigration. This scarcity occurred for several reasons: The earliest Chinese male immigrants considered themselves to be sojourners who would eventually return to China; the traditional role for Chinese women was to stay at home and care for children and aging parents; and the American frontier was considered too dangerous a place for Chinese women. As time passed, many Chinese men decided to put down roots and make a home in America. They wanted to start families or be reunited with existing families, but U.S. immigration laws discouraged the entry of Chinese women into the United States.

The earliest attempts to restrict immigration of Chinese women were laws prohibiting entry of prostitutes. Unfortunately, American immigration officials too often jumped to the conclusion that *all* Chinese women were prostitutes. Wives were submitted to bureaucratic red tape and humiliating interviews in which they were expected to prove their virtue.

The changing immigration laws and policies were a constant challenge to the Chinese American community. According to historian Xiaojian Zhao, "To Chinese immigrants, these laws were passed to separate families, reduce the Chinese population, and eventually rid the country of all Chinese. Finding a way to bring in new entries and establish families therefore became requirements for the community's survival."[9]

Chinese laborers who had entered the United States before the 1882 Exclusion Act was passed were not allowed to later bring in their wives because immigration officials had determined that the wives were actually "laborers" and, as such, were ineligible for immigration under the exclusion laws. Despite this obstacle, Chinese laborers continued to strive for reunification of their families. They worked and saved for years in order to buy enough property to qualify as merchants because merchants were among the few Chinese allowed to legally immigrate under the 1882 Exclusion Act, and because merchants could legally bring their wives and children with them to the United States. What had not yet been established during the exclusion era (1882–1943) was the right of an American citizen of Chinese ancestry to bring his Chinese-born wife to the United States. That right would be established in the case of *Tsoi Sim v. United States.*

The Case of Tsoi Sim

Tsoi Sim had been brought to the United States from China at the age of three by her laborer father. They entered the country prior to the passage of the 1882 Exclusion Act. Tsoi Sim grew up and attended school in California, never leaving the United States. Yet in 1902 Tsoi Sim was arrested and targeted for deportation under the Geary Act because she did not have a certificate of residence. The 1892 Geary Act had extended the 1882 Exclusion Act past its original ten years, while also adding the requirement that all Chinese immigrants register and carry a certificate of residence.

Before 1902 Tsoi Sim had married Yee Yuk Lum, a U.S. citizen by virtue of his birth on American soil—a status that had been established only a few years earlier in *Wong Kim Ark v. United States.* Tsoi Sim and her husband went to the District Court of Appeals, Ninth Circuit, and asked that she be allowed to stay with her American husband. In *Tsoi Sim v. United States*, issued in 1902, the court decided in Tsoi Sim's favor. The judge determined Tsoi Sim to be the lawful wife of an American citizen, and, under existing laws applying to married women, Tsoi Sim was entitled to live with her husband in his American domicile. The outcome of this important case was crucial to the establishment of Chinese families in America. According to Zhao,

> The ruling implied that any male American citizen of Chinese ancestry could go back to China, get married, and then bring his alien Chinese wife back to America, even if he was a laborer. After the 1906 earthquake and fire in San Francisco destroyed many of the city's civil documents, some Chinese immigrants falsely claimed U.S. citizenship by birth. They then used this claimed status to bring in their wives.[10]

The *Tsoi Sim* decision stood for two decades, and in that time many American families of Chinese descent were established.

The Immigration Act of 1924

The *Tsoi Sim* decision allowing a Chinese-born wife to stay in America with her Chinese American husband was overthrown by the passage of the Immigration Act of 1924. This act was purposefully designed to restrict immigrants from eastern, southern, and central Europe as well as from Asia and to favor immigrants from northern and western

Europe. The impact of the new immigration law on the Chinese community was immediate. Suddenly neither Chinese merchants nor Chinese Americans could bring their wives into the United States.

One person affected by the new law was American citizen Paul Yee. Yee, a U.S. native of Chinese ancestry, traveled to China in 1924 and married Chinese citizen Jee Shee. When Yee returned home to the United States with his bride later that year, he found that the newly enacted immigration law barred her entry. Jee Shee and thirty-four other Chinese brides attempting to land on U.S. soil won release on bond and were allowed to stay in the United States temporarily. This release was extended several times while a court challenge to the new immigration law was organized.

Chinese merchants immediately sued. In *Cheung Sum Shee et al. v. Nagle*, the U.S. Supreme Court ruled in favor of the Chinese merchants in 1925. The Court decided that because the merchants were in the United States to engage in trade, and therefore were not "immigrants," Chinese merchants could continue to bring their wives to America. In the same decision, the Court denied Chinese Americans the same right. Chinese-born spouses of Chinese Americans entered for the purpose of immigration, said the Court, yet Chinese immigrants were ineligible for naturalization according to earlier exclusion laws. The new Immigration Law of 1924 dictated that any alien ineligible for naturalized citizenship could not enter the country. Therefore, Chinese-born wives of American citizens were denied entry under the new law. In the Court's opinion, Justice James C. McReynolds pointed out that the Immigration Law of 1924 gave greater rights to Chinese merchants than to U.S. citizens. The remedy for this problem was in the legislature, not in the courts, suggested Justice McReynolds.

Zhao writes, "The Chinese American community burst

into an uproar upon learning the ramifications of the 1924 Immigration Act. The CCBA [Chinese Consolidated Benevolent Association] chapters in New York, Boston, and Seattle sent telegrams to the CCBA in San Francisco, urging the organization to take the lead in protesting the new law."[11] The Chinese benevolent associations joined with the Chinese American Citizens Alliance (CACA) and challenged the new law in court, emphasizing in their arguments that the legitimate rights of U.S. citizens were being denied.

When the court challenge failed, CACA developed a new strategy, and began heavily lobbying Congress to change the 1924 law. Again the Chinese Americans argued for reform on the basis of citizens' rights. Congress passed an amended immigration law in 1930 that allowed Chinese wives who had married before 1924 to enter the United States. The law's final version, however, gave these immigration rights only to Chinese Americans, not to all Americans. In the decade before World War II, there was considerable anti-Japanese feeling in America, and the legislature was unwilling to extend rights to all Americans for fear that Japanese Americans would make use of the relaxed immigration law.

Although the Chinese American challenge did not directly provide relief to other immigrant groups, Chinese Americans provided both a model of community political action by lobbying Congress for legislative relief from discriminatory acts and a vision of citizenship rights attainable by all Americans.

With the 1930 passage of the amended 1924 Immigration Act, Paul Yee's wife Jee Shee was finally granted legal resident status in the United States. During the intervening six years, Jee Shee had given birth to a son in Oakland, California, making her both the wife and mother of American citizens.

Equal Access to Education

Establishment of families meant that Chinese immigrant residents and Chinese Americans had yet another task before them—gaining equal access to public education for their children. As early as 1884, two Chinese immigrant residents of San Francisco sued the school board for the right to enroll their American-born child into the city's public school system. This struggle for access to education continued well into the twentieth century. Again, Chinese American successes in the courts resulted in expanded rights for all Americans.

In 1974 Kinney Kinomon Lau and twelve additional Chinese American students, none of whom spoke English, filed a class action lawsuit against Alan Nichols, president of the San Francisco Board of Education, on behalf of nearly three thousand Chinese-speaking students. The lawsuit declared that Chinese students could not follow classroom instruction that was given exclusively in English and that there were no adequate programs in the schools to help them learn English. English as a Second Language (ESL) programs were available only on a limited basis, and ESL instruction was restricted to forty minutes each day. The remainder of the instruction was in English, and bilingual teachers were very few in number.

A class action suit was filed only after the Chinese American community in San Francisco had exhausted all other means of relief. For several years, the students' parents had been deeply concerned about the failure of the school system to provide meaningful education for their children and had come to believe that the lack of bilingual education was discriminatory. In addition, Chinatown had seen an influx of immigrants in the 1960s, school dropout rates were up, and juvenile delinquency and crime rates were soaring. According to ethnic studies professor L. Ling-Chi Wang, Chinese American parents, convinced that

Chinese schoolchildren hold signs that display their Chinese names and their new, Americanized names.

their children were doomed "to become dropouts and to join the rolls of the unemployed," tried "innumerable meetings, heated negotiations, documented studies, peaceful and violent demonstrations, and concrete proposals to rectify the education deprivation suffered by the limited English-speaking Chinese American students."[12]

The U.S. Supreme Court ruled in the children's favor in a unanimous decision in *Lau v. Nichols* delivered in 1974. In the Court's written opinion, the judges ruled,

There is no equality of treatment merely by providing students with the same facilities, textbooks, teachers, and curriculum, for students who do not understand English are effectively foreclosed from any meaningful education. Basic English skills are at the very core of what these public schools teach. . . . It seems obvious that the

Chinese-speaking minority receive fewer benefits than the English-speaking majority from respondents' school system, which denies them a meaningful opportunity to participate in the educational program—all earmarks of the discrimination banned by the regulations. . . . Where inability to speak and understand the English language excludes national origin minority group children from effective participation in the educational program offered by a school district, the district must take affirmative steps to rectify the language deficiency in order to open its instructional program to these students.[13]

The Supreme Court ordered "appropriate relief" for the children. The ruling had the immediate effect of opening the door for the development of bilingual and bicultural education in all American public schools, not just San Francisco's. The ruling would have a direct impact on the lives of millions of school children. In addition, the ruling affected areas of law other than education. According to L. Ling-Chi Wang, "The Voters Rights Act of 1975 cited *Lau v. Nichols* as one of the bases for extending voting rights to non-English-speaking citizens."[14]

Chinese Immigrants and American Law

From their earliest days in America, Chinese immigrants used the American court system to fight discriminatory legislation and to seek inclusion under the equal protection clauses of American law. They fought to freely enter America, to work unimpeded, to bring their wives and children to the United States, to establish family and community life, and to have equal access to education. In their struggle to become Americans, the Chinese immigrants and Chinese Americans broadened the notion of civil rights to include all Americans, not just those of Chinese ancestry.

Notes

1. Quoted in Charles J. McClain and Laurene Wu McClain, "The Chinese Contribution to the Development of American Law," in Sucheng Chan, ed., *Entry Denied: Exclusion and the Chinese Community in America, 1882–1943*. Philadelphia: Temple University Press, 1991, p. 3.

2. McClain and McClain, "The Chinese Contribution to the Development of American Law," p. 11.

3. *Yick Wo v. Hopkins*, 1886.

4. McClain and McClain, "The Chinese Contribution to the Development of American Law," p. 15.

5. Erika Lee, *At America's Gates: Chinese Immigration During the Exclusion Era, 1882–1943*. Chapel Hill: University of North Carolina Press, 2003, p. 105.

6. Fourteenth Amendment to the U.S. Constitution.

7. Quoted in Lee, *At America's Gates*, p. 105.

8. Iris Chang, *The Chinese in America*. New York: Viking, 2003, p. 138.

9. Xiaojian Zhao, *Remaking Chinese America: Immigration, Family, and Community, 1940–1965*. New Brunswick, NJ: Rutgers University Press, 2002, p. 12.

10. Zhao, *Remaking Chinese America*, p. 14.

11. Zhao, *Remaking Chinese America*, p. 16.

12. L. Ling-Chi Wang, "*Lau v. Nichols:* History of a Struggle for Equal and Quality Education," in Charles J. McClain, ed., *Chinese Immigrants and American Law*. New York: Garland, 1994, p. 423.

13. *Lau v. Nichols*, 1974.

14. Wang, "*Lau v. Nichols*," p. 425.

CHAPTER 1

Coming to America

Why the Chinese Came to America

Barbara Lee Bloom

Although the Chinese emperors threatened their subjects with execution if they tried to emigrate from their homeland, thousands of peasants left China in the nineteenth century to seek their fortunes overseas. Barbara Lee Bloom, teacher of history at Champlain College in Burlington, Vermont, reviews the reasons why so many Chinese left home and traveled to America in this selection from her book *The Chinese Americans*. In the nineteenth century, China underwent a series of devastating events. First there was a series of intrusions by foreign powers and the introduction of addictive opium into China. When the corrupt and ineffective Qing dynasty attempted to resist those intrusions, the Chinese government lost both military battles and territory to Britain in the Opium Wars. Also, a civil war called the Taiping Rebellion broke out and caused even greater social and economic instability. Residents of southern China's Guangdong Province (where most of the foreign powers were based) were especially hurt by these events. When word came that gold had been discovered in America, the dream of economic success overseas became too compelling to ignore for many Chinese, and the first wave of immigration to the United States began.

For hundreds of years, Chinese rulers considered their vast empire the only civilized place in the world. By 214 B.C., the Chinese had built the Great Wall along China's western border to keep out "barbarians" (non-Chinese).

To the east, they were protected by thousands of miles of ocean. As a result, most Chinese knew little about what happened beyond their own shores, and fewer still cared. The Chinese remained isolated this way for centuries, with only occasional Europeans venturing into their lands.

From the sixteenth to the nineteenth century, though, colonial powers from Europe made attempts to trade with China. These efforts to establish commerce and diplomatic relations were rejected by the Chinese emperors, but the foreigners were determined to change that policy by force of arms if necessary. The Chinese lost the battles that followed, and the colonial powers forced the Chinese government to allow Europeans into the country. Ultimately, the entrance of these powers into China had a profound impact on the nation.

In the eyes of some Chinese, losing battles with foreigners meant that their government had grown weak. Others resented the corruption and power of the imperial court. In response, peasants revolted. However, these uprisings only weakened the government and country further. In addition, the fighting, whether against the colonial powers or the Chinese rebels, often destroyed farms and villages in the region near the South China Sea.

Guangdong Province

The people of Guangdong (Kwangtung) Province originated from pioneering tribes who moved southward as China's borders expanded. When they reached the South China Sea, they stopped traveling and established villages. Up until the nineteenth century, the rhythm of life in Guangdong remained almost unchanged. The people of this region spoke unique Cantonese dialects of Chinese. Most farmed the valleys; others planted crops on the terraced mountainsides; and fishermen caught fish and "farmed" the salt from the sea.

Here, as in all of China, the Chinese followed the teachings of Confucius, an ancient sage who preached respect for honest rulers, elders, and family. According to Confucianism, everyone from the poorest peasant to the emperor had a well-defined place in society. Farmers and laborers were held in higher esteem than merchants, and scholars were valued above all others. It was the duty of each son to look out for the well-being of his parents, and once a young man married, his wife, too, had an obligation to her husband's parents. Thus, for peasants in Guangdong, life centered around a large extended family, or clan, that made up an entire village. And because family was so important to the Chinese, they wrote their last name (their family's name) before their first. . . .

Guangdong remained a quiet rural province until the sixteenth century when Spanish, Dutch, Portuguese, and British merchants began arriving eager to trade for Chinese goods such as spices, porcelain, silk, and tea. Once the Chinese saw and became enamored with the European luxuries, the imperial government seemed helpless to stop its subjects from trading with the barbarians. Moreover, many men left their villages, becoming seamen on foreign vessels and emigrating overseas in search of wealth. . . .

Contact with Outsiders Increases

China's government disliked having its civilization contaminated by foreigners and their ideas. To keep its subjects at home, the Chinese government made emigration from China and contact with other countries a crime. As political scientist Kil Young Zo explains,

> The official attitude toward the emigrants was outright hostility, regarding all those who disappeared into, or appeared from, "lands beyond the sea," as potential rebels. An imperial edict of 1712 . . . declared that: "The Chinese government shall request foreign governments to

have those Chinese who have been abroad repatriated [sent back to China] so they may be executed."

Foreign governments, though, paid no attention to the edict and made no attempt to send immigrants back to China. In fact, European countries became more desirous of Chinese goods and more insistent with the passing years that China open itself to trade. As early as 1557, the Portuguese had established a fortified trading post at Macao, an island off the coast of Guangdong. By the eighteenth century, other colonial powers came from Europe, and it

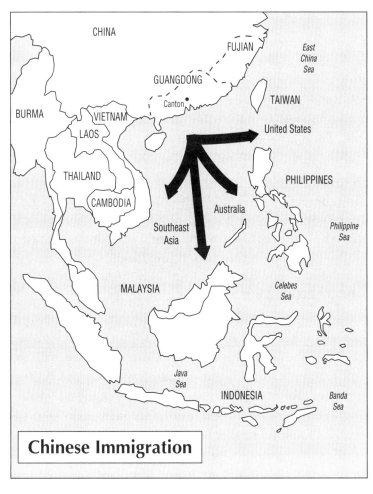

Chinese Immigration

became obvious they would use any means possible, even force if necessary, to take what they wanted. So in 1757, Chinese emperor Qian Long was coerced into opening the port of Canton, the capital of the province, for international trade.

The result was an influx of Europeans and their ideas. Traders, merchants, and Western missionaries entered China. . . .

As missionaries brought Christianity, trade with Europeans brought prosperity to the region. Farmers learned to grow new vegetables from abroad such as sweet potatoes and yams, which thrived in the mild climate of southern China. The nation's merchants and tradesmen discovered new markets for Chinese goods, and craftsmen found new buyers for their wares. With new prosperity flowing into the region, the population steadily grew.

The growth in population, though, soon became a burden. Peasant farmers divided up their land among their sons until, by the nineteenth century, many plots had become too small to support a family. Furthermore, Guangdong was a tropical region where monsoon rains often led to disastrous floods. During the few dry years, drought killed almost all the crops, creating food shortages throughout the overpopulated province.

The Opium Wars

More than just small farms and insufficient food brought misery to the people of Guangdong. The outbreak of war added to the hardships of the peasants. The cause of the conflict was opium, an addicting drug that the British hoped to exchange for Chinese goods. The Chinese government imposed high tariffs on British goods to keep them out, but English merchants smuggled in opium, which they acquired from their colony in India. The emperor quickly saw how opium's addicting potential could destroy the productivity of his subjects; as the Chinese used opium, they got addicted and were less able to concentrate on their jobs, farms, and families. The importation of the drug was ultimately banned by a decree from the emperor, but the British defied the decree, continuing to smuggle in opium.

A confrontation soon followed. The emperor sent a commissioner, a representative of the imperial court, to Canton. The commissioner went to the docks, ordered the opium chests removed, and demanded the drug be burned. Then he had the ashes floated on the river as an offering to the deities. Angry at the loss of the valuable cargo, England retaliated, using their guns and military might to defeat China in the First Opium War, lasting from 1839 to 1842. The Second Opium War involved the French as well as the British and ended in 1857.

The treaties signed after these wars forced China to open five of its ports to foreign trade, and to cede the island of Hong Kong to the British. England also demanded that China render monetary compensation for the damages to English ships and property caused during the war. In turn, to cover payments to the British, the imperial government raised taxes on the land. It fell to the people of Guangdong, on whose soil the war had been fought, to pay about 70 percent of the reparations for the First Opium War. Furthermore, the opium, which the British were now free to import to China, drained currency away from the province; profits went to English rather than Chinese merchants. This made prices on purchased goods rise, and everything became more expensive than before. . . .

The Taiping Rebellion and Clan Wars

Although some Chinese believed that their troubles were because of the evil foreigners, others blamed their own government and the corruption that had befallen Manchu leaders of the Qing dynasty. After the First Opium War, discontent with the government increased, and peasants revolted against the imperial court in 1851. Demanding reform, Hong Xiuquan, a farmer, led rebels in an uprising against the Qing dynasty. Known as the Taiping Rebellion, the fighting lasted thirteen years before the emperor's troops finally subdued the rebels. The peasants, though, had almost succeeded in overthrowing the government and, in doing so, had greatly weakened the emperor's authority.

In addition to the battles of the Taiping Rebellion, local clan wars broke out and made life miserable in Guangdong. Because of the fighting, many families found their homes and villages lying in ruins and their crops burned, and they became desperate. In the face of such desperate circumstances, men anxious to support their families began to leave on ships from Canton, Hong Kong, and Macao in search of work abroad. The emigrants planned to stay away only three to five years and then return home with enough money to rebuild their homes and lead prosperous lives. These men became known in their villages as sojourners, or temporary residents, for none of them imagined they would stay away from China forever.

The Call of Foreign Lands

By the mid–nineteenth century, sojourners had several destinations to choose from. In 1841, a Chinese scholar named Wei Yun had written *The Geography of the World*, a series of books that told a great deal about the territories and nations beyond China's borders. Many Chinese were now curious about the people in other places and how they lived; Wei's descriptions excited them. He told of northern Mexico and California, calling these places golden lands with an abundance of birds and animals. Farmers there, Wei wrote, had thousands of sheep and cows. For many Chinese, this region seemed like a place where a hardworking man could succeed. . . .

As Chinese men considered going abroad as a means of finding employment and earning money to help their families, tales of fabulous riches to be made in California reached them. Anthropologist Mary Coolidge explains, "The news of the discovery of gold in the Sacramento Valley [California] in January, 1848, reached Hong Kong in the spring and created much excitement there."

With the discovery of gold and the desire of many to reach the goldfields of California, ship captains saw the chance to make a lot of money by charging high prices for passage. They used any means they could to lure young men to their ships. As Coolidge writes,

> Masters of foreign vessels afforded every facility to emigration, distributing placards, maps and pamphlets with highly colored accounts of the Golden Hills, and reaping enormous profits as the demand for passages and freight increased. In 1850 forty-four vessels left Hong Kong for California with nearly 500 passengers and by the end of 1851 it was estimated that there were 25,000 Chinese in California engaged either in . . . mining or in domestic and manual labor.

Despite the tales of riches to be made abroad, the decision to leave China was often a hard choice. During the 1840s, life in the United States was unknown to most Chinese. Almost no one in China knew for certain what lay across the sea. Men worried about leaving their wives and families behind, and few could be sure when or if they would return.

Even though they faced the unknown, as more tales circulated about California, daring young men saw opportunity awaiting them abroad.

The Chinese Experience in Nineteenth-Century America

Shih-Shan Henry Tsai

The men who left southern China to immigrate to the United States in the nineteenth century typically traveled by boat down the Pearl River Delta to Hong Kong or Macao and then bought passage on a steamship to America. After arriving at Gold Mountain (the immigrants' term for America), the men sought work in a variety of occupations, most prominently in gold rush mining camps and on the transcontinental railroad. In this selection from *The Chinese Experience in America*, Shih-Shan Henry Tsai explains the credit arrangements immigrants made to buy passage to America and notes the harsh and dangerous conditions that the Chinese encountered while working in American mines and on the railroad. Tsai also describes the "Chinatowns" that grew up in urban areas of the American West. These ethnic enclaves made possible the continuance of Chinese culture in America, although they also had a darker side that included opium use, gambling, and prostitution. Tsai is professor of history and director of the Asian Studies program at the University of Arkansas, Fayetteville. He is also the author of several books on Chinese history, including *Perpetual Happiness: The Ming Emperor Yongle.*

Chinese immigrants to Gum Sann, or the "Gold Mountain" of California, usually traveled in junks, lorchas [a light vessel], or rafts over the waterways of the Pearl River

Shih-Shan Henry Tsai, *The Chinese Experience in America*. Bloomington: Indiana University Press, 1986. Copyright © 1986 by Shih-Shan Henry Tsai. All rights reserved. Reproduced by permission of the publisher.

Delta from their native villages to Hong Kong or Macao, then took a steamship for the trans-Pacific voyage. American and British ship masters afforded a variety of facilities to accommodate the immigrants, then charged them high passenger rates, ranging from $40 to $50 one way and $60 to $70 for a round trip. During 1852, about 30,000 Chinese embarked at Hong Kong for San Francisco and paid a total of approximately $1,300,000 for the voyages. At the beginning of 1856, the Reverend William Speer calculated that Chinese immigrants to California had paid a total $2,329,580 for trans-Pacific trips. Understandably, transportation companies became powerful supporters of Chinese immigration. In 1866 the Pacific Mail Steamship Company entered the China trade, and a little later the Occidental and Oriental Steamship Company was organized as a competitor. During the peak years of the Chinese immigration, from 1876 to 1890, steamships carried an estimated 200,000 Chinese to West Coast ports and over half that number back to China where they visited or remained. American and British companies probably realized more than $11 million in steerage ticket fees.

Some emigrants were able to put up enough cash for the passage fees; others who were poor and could not raise the necessary money usually entered a "credit ticket agreement." The Wells-Fargo Bank History Room in San Francisco displays a contract, signed in 1849 between an English company in Shanghai and a group of Chinese laborers, that illustrates how the credit system worked. From the time the workers left Shanghai, the expenses for their provisions and transportation were defrayed by the company. On arriving in San Francisco, the company was obligated to seek employment for the Chinese mechanics and laborers; the money the company had advanced would be returned when employment was secured. A moiety [indefinite portion] of each immigrant's wages would be deducted monthly until the debt, which amounted to $120 each, was absorbed. After that, the Chinese would receive their wages in full every month. . . .

A typical Chinese immigrant wore coarse gray, wide-legged trousers, a broad-brimmed straw hat, and a pair of sandals or wooden shoes. The few merchants who joined the gold rush usually wore silk caps, mandarin-style gowns, and cloth shoes. During the trans-Pacific voyage, which took between two and three months, he used his rationed water to brew hot tea, and ate lemon peel or salted, dried plums to prevent scurvy and seasickness. Together with his fellow passengers, he was crowded into the steerage of the ship and spent most of his time dozing in his narrow cot. When his ship arrived in San Francisco or Eureka, he wadded his body with personal belongings and brought his small bundle of clothing and blankets with him. After clearing the dreaded customs house, he was met by a Chinese representative who registered his name and sent him to join his provincials in some sort of caravansary [large inn] boardinghouse. There the weary immigrant could rest and arrange for a portion of his wages to be remitted home periodically to his relatives in China. He also immediately arranged for his body to be shipped to China for burial in case he should meet with an accident in America; he believed that if his body was buried in a strange land, untended by his family, his soul would never stop wandering in the darkness of the other world. After taking care of such details, he left for the gold mine, railway construction site, or marshy field, in express wagons or on foot.

Work in the Mines

During the early days of the gold rushes a cosmopolitan assortment of humanity gathered on the mining frontiers of the American West, including white Americans, British subjects, Germans, French, Indians, Mexicans, Spaniards,

Negroes, and Chinese. By the 1860s, when the gold bonanza yielded only modest pay dirt, most of the white miners had forsaken the gulches and canyons, but the Chinese stayed on and made up almost two-thirds of the mining labor force in the states west of the Rocky Mountains. The United States census of 1870 counted 17,069 Chinese miners, more than 11 percent of the total 152,107 in the country. But in the western states, the number of the Chinese miners was very significant. For example, of Oregon's 3,965 miners, 2,428 or 61.2 percent were Chinese; in Montana, of 6,720 miners, 1,415, about 21 percent, were Chinese; in Idaho, among the 6,579 miners, 3,853 or 58.6 percent were Chinese; and out of the 36,339 California mining laborers, 9,087 or 25 percent came from China. According to mining expert Henry Degroot, during the period 1849–1870 the value of the precious metals produced upon the Pacific coast approximated $1.2 billion, and in 1871 alone Chinese miners extracted and put into circulation something over $27 million. . . .

Like other prospectors, Chinese miners used the pickaxe, the pan, the sluice box, and the water wheel, known in America as the China pump, to work the gravel heaps and tailings of the mines. Living conditions in the mining camps were primitive and often unsanitary. At the camp site, workers slept in small tents, on the ground, or huddled together in cabins or tents abandoned by the whites. Some of them even burrowed caves, using a blanket to cover them. They retained their blue cotton tunics and broad trousers, their wooden shoes and broad-brimmed hats with a queue, or pigtail, hanging down their backs. Since most Chinese spoke little or no English, those who worked for American companies were usually hired through a broker who would recruit miners from among his relatives or fellow villagers. The employer would pay a lump sum to the broker who provided the daily necessities and dispensed wages to his crew. This system was also practiced for hiring in railroad construction, wheat harvesting, and in the canneries.

Chinese miners were particularly subject to danger from the lawless outcasts attracted to the camps. They were also confronted with discrimination in the form of confiscatory taxes and other legal obstructions. For example, the Oregon Constitutional Convention in August, 1857, ruled that Chinese should not be allowed to own mining claims or land. Two years later, when Oregon achieved statehood, its legislature levied a $5 poll tax on every Chinese. In 1864, Washington Territory passed an act designed to disfranchise the Chinese in the mining field. A special quarterly capitation tax of $6, called the "Chinese Police Tax," was levied on every "Mongolian" in the territory. The sheriff in each county was responsible for collecting the tax and was entitled to keep 25 percent of the money he collected. Moreover, if there were disputes between whites and Chinese, the latter were prohibited from giving testimony in the courts. In Montana, Nevada, and Idaho, similar discriminations were imposed on the Chinese, while the California legislature, beginning in 1852, passed a series of laws against the Chinese miners. The Act of 1855 required the owner of a vessel to pay $450 for each passenger who was ineligible for citizenship and the Act of 1862 required a monthly payment of $2.50 by each "Mongolian" over eighteen who had not paid the miner's license fee.

The intent of these various tax measures seemingly was to protect white miners against competition from the Chinese and to discourage the immigration of the Chinese. Such official restrictions probably encouraged white men's contempt for and violence against their Chinese counterparts. The yellow skins, strange features, small figures, and incomprehensible language of the Chinese led whites to believe that the Chinese were an inferior race. White jail-birds, gamblers, deserters, desperadoes, thieves, and frequently even respected citizens used such epithets as "John Chinaman," "Chink Chinamen," or "heathen," when they talked to the Chinese, refusing to address them by name. During the anti-Chinese movement of the late 1870s and 1880s, labor unions further propagated the myth of the inferiority of the Orientals. But in spite of adversity, the Chinese doggedly pursued their right to stand beside other miners as equal partners. They resisted the collection of these confiscatory and clearly discriminatory taxes. Most of these acts were later declared unconstitutional by state or federal courts. . . .

Work on the Railroad

The one employer of Chinese who most enhanced their reputation as good and reliable workers was the Central Pacific Railway Company. Incorporated on June 28, 1861, it was controlled by four Sacramento merchants—Leland Stanford, Collis P. Huntington, Mark Hopkins, and Charles Crocker. These fortune-builders realized that the best means to conquer and exploit the great American West was by railroad construction. They knew that public enthusiasm for railroad-building was at its height and that even the enemies of the railroad could not deny its importance.

As the government at all levels thrust credit and resources upon the railroad-promoters, the Central Pacific and the Union Pacific, by a Congressional act in 1862, were chartered to build the first American transcontinental railroad. The former was to start work in Sacramento and push its way eastward through the Sierra Nevada Range while the latter was to start from Omaha and work westward until it joined with the Central Pacific. By 1866, the two companies had begun a race to secure the largest possible federal subsidy. The Central Pacific had a more formidable task because its track had to cross the Sierra

Nevada—a solid wall of granite—and the arid plains and deserts of Nevada and Utah. Shortly after Congress approved the project, the Central Pacific formed a subsidiary company called Crocker and Company, to take over construction contracts; but after two years, less than fifty miles of track had been laid. Crocker and his associates realized that each week lost meant the loss of hundreds of thousands of dollars in land and cash subsidies and that whichever road reached Salt Lake Basin first would probably come to dominate the entire system. They also were aware that while their construction was bogged down because of climatic and engineering difficulties, the rival Union Pacific could build two-thirds of its road before encountering any appreciable engineering problems. Under these circumstances Crocker and Company decided, in early 1865, to draw on the Chinese for its labor supply.

When the decision to hire Chinese was made known, Crocker's European employees, including his superintendent, James Harvey Strobridge, protested that the Chinese were too small and frail to take on heavy construction jobs and that they were not fit to become masons or to handle explosives. Crocker was said to have reminded his skeptics that the Chinese had built the biggest masonry structure in the world—the Great Wall of China—and had invented gunpowder, introducing Westerners to its uses. Strobridge first agreed to try fifty Chinese, using them to cut down trees, root out stumps, break and cart rocks, and lay down rails and ties. The results were so gratifying that Strobridge agreed to accept fifty more and, by the spring of 1865, more Chinese were employed by the Central Pacific. . . .

The Chinese were hired in groups of fifty to a hundred, and as practiced in the mining industry, their broker received the wages for the group in monthly lump sums. On average, a white laborer was paid $35 a month plus board and lodging; a Chinese laborer, however, received between

$26 and $35 per month and had to provide his own food and housing. The broker furnished his workers with supplies of food and supplied a cook to prepare meals, make tea, and keep a large boiler of hot water for the group's bathing. The Chinese menu included pork, poultry, rice, bean sprouts, bamboo shoots, various kinds of vegetables, dried fruit and fish, Chinese sausage, and peanut oil, some of which were imported directly from Hong Kong and Canton. The workday began at sunrise and ended at sunset, six days a week. They spent Sundays doing laundry, mending, talking, smoking, and gambling. By the end of the month, the broker deducted all the expenses that had been defrayed, then distributed earnings to each individual. Most Chinese laborers probably saved around $20 a month.

The quality of Chinese rail workers was severely tested when the railhead had to cross the Sierra Nevada Range. Often ridges jutted up from the valley floors below; in the winter heavy snows made sure deathtraps for anyone in an exposed area. In the spring of 1866, when assaulting Cape Horn Mountain, the Chinese devised a solution to a difficult tunnelling problem. They wove reeds into large wicker baskets which were hauled to the top of the cliffs where one or two Chinese got inside. By a pulley system, they were then lowered over cliffs two thousand feet above the base of the American River Canyon. They chiseled holes through the granite escarpments, scrambled up the lines and placed the dynamite and lit it before they were pulled up to the top of the cliff, usually just in time to escape the explosion. A white foreman with a gang of 30 to 40 Chinese generally constituted the work force at each end of a tunnel.

Central Pacific records indicate that Chinese workers advanced the railroad an average of 1.18 feet daily and that sometimes it took 300 Chinese ten days just to clear and grub a mile of roadbed. Climbing through the High Sierra was difficult enough, but working in the freezing cold of the winter season made it even more dangerous. Accidents and severe weather took a heavy toll among the Chinese laborers. A good many died when baskets were not pulled up fast enough or a rope broke. Uncounted numbers froze to death when unexpected blizzards caused shelters, often old barns or wooden sheds, to collapse. Many who were covered by snow slides were not found until the next spring when the snow melted. It was estimated that more than 1,200 Chinese perished before the golden spike was driven at Promontory junction in Utah.[1]

Chinese Culture Transplanted to America

The Chinese who came to America in the late nineteenth century were mainly poor peasants and workers who had to struggle to survive in the destitute circumstances of their times. The well-to-do Chinese gentry class—scholars, officials, and landowners—were the elite of Chinese society and had no need to leave their ancestral homes to pan for gold or to work in rail gangs in a distant land. But whether they were poor or rich, the Chinese rarely abandoned their homeland to search for another. When they went abroad, a wife and children frequently were left behind. Almost all emigrants hoped to return after having accumulated a fortune by trade or by labor in a foreign country. In America a Chinese laborer who could save up a few hundred dollars would consider it a small fortune and would usually retire to his native village in Guangdong. He could expect to spend his declining years surrounded by his filial sons and grandchildren, and when he died be laid to rest among the honored dead of a long ancestral line. Such a "situation-centered" Chinese culture, as cultural anthropologist Francis L.K. Hsu has called it, is quite different from the "individual-centered" Ameri-

1. The two track sections were joined in 1869, completing the transcontinental railroad.

can culture. This cultural gulf was the source of much of
the subsequent friction between Chinese immigrants and
white Americans.

In spite of their strong ties to the homeland, Chinese
immigrants did not establish a miniature replica of traditional Chinese society in America. They lived in an ab-
normal society full of young males, wandering sojourners,
whose dream was to put in a few years of hard labor and to
return home wealthy and respected "Gold Mountain
Guests." This "sojourner's mentality" had deep roots in
Chinese cultural tradition. Nineteenth-century China was
an unsophisticated agrarian society. The great majority of
the Chinese people still embraced both Confucianism and
Taoism, religious systems which, to a great extent, reflected the inspirations and aspirations of peasants. A typical peasant, who lived in a small rural village, rarely traveled, and had insufficient knowledge of geography to go
far unless he was directed or accompanied by someone
else. He idolized Lao Tze's [ancient Chinese philosopher]
famed Utopia in which "the next place might be so near at
hand that one could hear the cocks crowing in it, the dogs
barking; but the people would grow old and die without
ever having been there." He observed Confucian filial duties as binding restrictions: "While father and mother are
alive, a good son does not wander far afield." Emigration
was generally looked upon as banishment, a severe punishment next only to death. Out of these beliefs grew the
concept of sojourning, an idea that stressed the temporary
nature of one's absence from home.

The Chinese sojourner's society in America was
markedly different from the home country in two ways.
First, the population was almost totally transient and, second, there was a great scarcity of females. Mainly because
of the seasonal or temporary nature of available work,
there was scarcely a Chinese laborer in America who had

not lived in several places along the coast. The fluidity of Chinese society was best demonstrated by the phenomenal increase in the Chinese population in the 1870s and by the fact that every year hundreds of Chinese returned to their native land because of seasonal unemployment. As a result, relatively few Chinese owned property, real or personal, in America, a situation that often led to the complaint of American local governments that the Chinese did not pay a fair share of taxes.

Chinatowns

This social instability also made possible the rise of Chinese quarters or Chinatowns in American cities. In the late 1870s, between one-fifth and one-fourth of all Chinese in the United States were in San Francisco; most of them resided in seven or eight blocks of that city. The situation was more or less the same in Sacramento and in other urban communities. In these small and often crowded quarters, the Chinese built temples and public halls, established stores and businesses, and opened restaurants and wash houses. They retained their native customs and formed a nation within a nation; a tendency characteristic of all immigrant groups in America. The men continued to wear their hair in queues—a peculiar hairstyle imposed on them since the seventeenth century by their Manchu conquerers—while most of their women practiced the tradition of foot-binding. They also retained their national habits in food, reading, and mode of life. . . .

Life in Chinatown was bustling, noisy, and colorful. A typical street included signs advertising fortune tellers, barber shops, butcher shops, doctors' clinics, and a variety of stores. For a few cents, a fortune-teller would predict a customer's destiny, dissect the characters forming the customer's name, or read his palms. For a few more cents, the fortune-teller could even decipher the "eight diagrams"[2] for his customer and could conjure up his dead relatives to talk with him. Not far from the fortune-teller was a barber shop, whose trade emblem was a washstand and basin placed just outside the doors. On the same block, Chinese doctors and druggists abounded. Some specialized in feeling the pulse and disbursing herbal prescriptions; others claimed to be experts in curing wounds and fixing broken bones. Inside a typical Chinatown store were scrolls hanging on the walls and Chinese characters written upon red papers which were pasted on doors or over money chests. On the scrolls were quotations from the classics and famous poets, while on the red papers were popular rhymed verse, such as "Wealth Arising Like Bubbling Spring," and "Customers Coming Like Clouds." Chinese merchants and customers frequently began their bargaining with polite conversations about the quality of the scrolls and the philosophical meaning of the verses.

The Dark Side of the Old Chinatowns

Most Chinatowns also included narrow streets or alleys given over to shabby apartments, dens for opium smoking, gambling joints, and brothels. From these unsanitary areas came the Chinese criminals; their existence had an important negative impact on the image of the broader Chinese community. According to San Francisco police records, which are probably typical, during the period from 1879 to 1910, Chinese arrested on criminal charges constituted 8.8 percent of all arrests. Of the Chinese arrested, only 11 out of 100 were convicted, the majority for violations of municipal health and fire ordinances. The San Francisco Board of Health was controlled by anti-Chinese physicians who credited "Chinatown with introducing and disseminating every epidemic outbreak to hit San Francisco." To them, Chinatown was

2. The diagrams symbolize eight natural phenomena and are the basic constituents of the I Ching divination system.

more than a slum, it was "a laboratory of infection, peopled by lying and treacherous aliens who had minimal regard for the health of the American people." But Dr. Joan B. Trauner has argued that the pronouncements by the Board of Health were often characterized by political and social expedience, rather than by social insight. The Chinese were made medical scapegoats in San Francisco.

Chinese wage earners, while holding or looking for jobs, usually sought temporary accommodation in the most inexpensive place possible. It was not uncommon for 15 or 20 bachelors to share a small room. In San Francisco's Globe Hotel in the 1860s, some 300 to 400 transient Chinese laborers were housed in extremely congested conditions, highlighting for the authorities their housing problems. In 1870, the California legislature passed a "Cubic Air" law which required a lodging house to provide at least 500 cubic feet of clear atmosphere for each adult person in an apartment. When the Chinese landlords and lodgers resisted complying with the law they were put into prison *en masse*. Later, the Cubic Air Board adopted the notorious "Queue Ordinance" whereby every male prisoner was required to have his hair cut by a clipper to a uniform length of one inch from the scalp. In carrying out the ordinance, a San Francisco policeman named Matthew Noonan cut the queue of Ho Ah-kow, a Chinese prisoner, to the very inch prescribed in the ordinance. The Circuit Court in California in 1879 ruled that the ordinance was unconstitutional and that Ho be awarded a $10,000 compensation by Noonan and the San Francisco city government.

Gambling and Opium

In addition to housing-ordinance violations, Chinatowns were notorious gambling havens. The most common forms of Chinese gambling were fan-tan and lottery. Fan-tan players guessed the exact coins or cards left under a cup after the pile of cards had been counted off four at a time. Fan-tan later became very popular among the Japanese and Filipinos; some lost all their hard-earned money before they could return to their native lands. The same consequences befell many a Chinese worker; many were so impoverished they could not pay for their ashes to be sent to their native villages in China for permanent burial. The lottery game was also known as the white dover card sweepstakes. Any person who wished to enter the game bought a randomly assigned sweepstakes number. In the lottery saloons, about ten of which existed in 1868, drawings were held twice a day; and the odds of winning were probably about the same as in modern-day "keno" in a Las Vegas casino. Many white Americans were attracted to the lotteries; but the unquestioned winners were the saloon owners. There are indications that the gambling-house operators received protection from corrupt police officers. In his testimony before the California Senate Committee in 1876, a Chinese witness estimated that there were about 200 Chinese gambling houses in San Francisco and probably a dozen in Sacramento. He indicated that fan-tan gambling operators were required to pay police officers $5 in "hush money" each week and lottery owners $8 a month for the privilege of keeping their businesses open.

Another factor that contributed to a negative Chinatown image was opium smoking. Originally introduced to China by English merchants from India in the late eighteenth century, this vice not only drained gold and silver out of China but enfeebled the Chinese population and demoralized their society. When pressed by the English to legalize the opium trade, the Chinese Emperor Daoguang (1821–1850) was reported to have vehemently exclaimed: "I know that wicked and designing men, for purpose of lust and profit, will clandestinely introduce the poisonous drug, but nothing under heaven shall ever induce me to legalize the certain ruin of my people." Chinese refusal to legalize the opium trade ultimately led to the infamous Opium War, in which China suffered her first defeat at the hands of a European nation. But the war did not solve the opium issue and for several years opium was not contraband in the newly annexed British colony of Hong Kong, from where the Chinese carried opium into the United States. . . .

Prostitution

Another Chinatown social evil, prostitution, was exacerbated by the shortage of Chinese women in America. . . . This skewed sex ratio of the Chinese population existed even in Hawaii; there, in 1890, of the 16,752 Chinese, only 1,409 were females and, in 1900, among the 25,767 Chinese, only 3,471 were females. "There were more monks than rice porridge," as the Chinese described the situation; prostitution was inevitable.

Prostitution, the world's oldest profession, was, of course, not a unique Chinese vice. All seriously deprived classes in American society have been plagued by this evil. But anti-Chinese agitators in the late nineteenth century nonetheless held the Chinese particularly culpable. They charged that Chinese prostitutes, who demanded less money for their services, spread the practice among young white males, exerting a bad influence on the entire community. Whether such charges were true or not, government investigations made clear that the Chinese were not solely responsible. Prostitutes received protection from corrupt policemen and other officials and could not have operated without such cooperation.

Chinese prostitutes were mostly imported from Hong Kong and held under contract by underworld figures. The Reverend Otis Gibson, who provided shelter for runaway Chinese prostitutes, testified in 1876 before a special Congressional committee that he had seen some of the contracts and found them to be replete with false promises and outright fraud. Once in America, the girls were quartered in the small alleys of Chinatowns, notably on Jackson Street of San Francisco and I Street of Sacramento. They lived in small filthy rooms of 10 by 10 or 12 by 12 feet. If the girls failed to attract customers, or refused to receive company because of illness or other reasons, they were beaten with sticks. When such punishment did not work, the house mistress tortured them in a variety of sadistic and cruel ways. A great many, terrified by such savage treatment, ran away before the expiration of their contracts. Some slipped back to China, others went to the country for temporary hiding; the most fortunate found shelter in the Gibson station-house. However, countless numbers of unfortunate girls were passed from owner to owner, never escaping their vicious captivity.

It was impossible to ascertain the exact number of the Chinese prostitutes in America. Conservative estimates put the figure between 1,500 and 2,000 in 1870, but a Chinese official who visited California in 1876 reported that there were approximately 6,000 Chinese women in the United States and that 80 to 90 percent were "daughters of joy." Although some municipal laws were passed and sporadic enforcement measures were taken, the problems remained, mainly from police corruption and the ease with which brothels were moved from place to place. Since there was no local supply of Chinese women, some reformers hoped to end the evil by cutting off the supply from Hong Kong and other Chinese ports. Consequently, in 1875 the United States Congress passed the Page Law to stop women "of disreputable character" from coming to America. Nevertheless, pimps continued to find ways to elude the authorities, and prostitution, like opium, remained a problem in Chinatowns.

In order to protect the interests of brothel owners, an

association of Chinese villains, known in San Francisco as "the highbinders," was formed. The highbinders, who lived off the prostitutes by levying upon each girl a weekly fee, left behind them a trail of mayhem, blackmail, and murder. It was this lawless element in Chinese society which led many Americans, such as Frank M. Pixley, spokesman for the municipality of San Francisco, to conclude: "I believe that the Chinese have no souls to save, and if they have, they are not worth saving." Pixley's ethnocentric view of the Chinese was typical of nineteenth-century America; it was echoed in a special Congressional committee report: "Upon the point of morals, there is no Aryan or European race which is not far superior to the Chinese as a class." Of course, such racist expressions were not unlike those of the chauvinistic mandarins who, as late as the 1870s, continued to call the Europeans and Americans "Western barbarians."

Danger and Death: Building the Transcontinental Railroad

Maxine Hong Kingston

Maxine Hong Kingston, California-born daughter of immigrants from southern China, describes in her imagina-
tive works *Woman Warrior* and *China Men* the experience
of her grandparents and parents in America. In this selection from *China Men*, Kingston relates the story of her
grandfather Ah Goong as he carries out the dangerous
work of building the transcontinental railroad. Chinese
railroad workers faced the constant threat of injury and
death from gunpowder and dynamite explosions, falls from
high mountain cliffs, and freezing in blizzards. Kingston,
Chancellor's Distinguished Professor at the University of
California, Berkeley, won the American Book Award in
1981 for *China Men*.

When cliffs, sheer drops under impossible overhangs,
ended the road, the [Chinese railroad] workers filled the
ravines or built bridges over them. They climbed above the
site for tunnel or bridge and lowered one another down in
wicker baskets made stronger by the lucky words they had
painted on four sides. Ah Goong got to be a basketman because he was thin and light. Some basketmen were fifteen-

Maxine Hong Kingston, *China Men*. New York: Knopf, 1980. Copyright © 1977 by
Maxine Hong Kingston. Reproduced by permission.

year-old boys. He rode the basket barefoot, so his boots, the kind to stomp snakes with, would not break through the bottom. The basket swung and twirled, and he saw the world sweep underneath him; it was fun in a way, a cold new feeling of doing what had never been done before. Suspended in the quiet sky, he thought all kinds of crazy thoughts, that if a man didn't want to live any more, he could just cut the ropes or, easier, tilt the basket, dip, and never have to worry again. He could spread his arms and the air would momentarily hold him before he fell past the buzzards, hawks, and eagles, and landed impaled on the tip of a sequoia. This high and he didn't see any gods, no Cowboy, no Spinner [Chinese names of stars]. He knelt in the basket though he was not bumping his head against the sky. Through the wickerwork, slivers of depths darted like needles, nothing between him and air but thin rattan. Gusts of wind spun the light basket. "Aiya," said Ah Goong. Winds came up under the basket, bouncing it. Neighboring baskets swung together and parted. He and the man next to him looked at each other's faces. They laughed. They might as well have gone to Malaysia to collect bird nests. Those who had done high work there said it had been worse; the birds screamed and scratched at them. Swinging near the cliff, Ah Goong stood up and grabbed it by a twig. He dug holes, then inserted gunpowder and fuses. He worked neither too fast nor too slow, keeping even with the others. The basketmen signaled one another to light the fuses. He struck match after match and dropped the burnt matches over the sides. At last his fuse caught; he waved, and the men above pulled hand over hand hauling him up, pulleys creaking. The scaffolds stood like a row of gibbets. Gallows trees along a ridge. "Hurry, hurry," he said. Some impatient men clambered up their ropes. Ah Goong ran up the ledge road they'd cleared and watched the explosions, which banged almost synchronously, echoes booming like war. He moved his scaffold to the next section of cliff and went down in the basket again, with bags of dirt, and set the next charge.

Explosions and Falls

This time two men were blown up. One knocked out or killed by the explosion fell silently, the other screaming, his arms and legs struggling. A desire shot out of Ah Goong for an arm long enough to reach down and catch them. Much time passed as they fell like plummets. The shreds of baskets and a cowboy hat skimmed and tacked. The winds that pushed birds off course and against mountains did not carry men. Ah Goong also wished that the conscious man would fall faster and get it over with. His hands gripped the ropes, and it was difficult to let go and get on with the work. "It can't happen twice in a row," the basketmen said the next trip down. "Our chances are very good. The trip after an accident is probably the safest one." They raced to their favorite basket, checked and double-checked the four ropes, yanked the strands, tested the pulleys, oiled them, reminded the pulleymen about the signals, and entered the sky again.

Another time, Ah Goong had been lowered to the bottom of a ravine, which had to be cleared for the base of a trestle, when a man fell, and he saw his face. He had not died of shock before hitting bottom. His hands were grabbing at air. His stomach and groin must have felt the fall all the way down. At night Ah Goong woke up falling, though he slept on the ground, and heard other men call out in their sleep. No warm women tweaked their ears and hugged them. "It was only a falling dream," he reassured himself.

Across a valley, a chain of men working on the next mountain, men like ants changing the face of the world, fell, but it was very far away. Godlike, he watched men whose faces he could not see and whose screams he did not hear roll and bounce and slide like a handful of sprinkled gravel.

After a fall, the buzzards circled the spot and reminded the workers for days that a man was dead down there. The men threw piles of rocks and branches to cover bodies from sight. . . .

Introduction of Dynamite

In the third year of pounding granite by hand, a demon invented dynamite. The railroad workers were to test it. They had stopped using gunpowder in the tunnels after avalanches, but the demons said that dynamite was more precise. They watched a scientist demon mix nitrate, sulphate, and glycerine, then flick the yellow oil, which exploded off his fingertips. Sitting in a meadow to watch the dynamite detonated in the open, Ah Goong saw the men in front of him leap impossibly high into the air; then he felt a shove as if from a giant's unseen hand—and he fell backward. The boom broke the mountain silence like fear breaking inside stomach and chest and groin. No one had gotten hurt; they stood up laughing and amazed, looking around at how they had fallen, the pattern of the explosion. Dynamite was much more powerful than gunpowder. Ah Goong had felt a nudge, as if something kind were moving him out of harm's way. "All of a sudden I was sitting next to you." "Aiya. If we had been nearer, it would have killed us." "If we were stiff, it would have gone through us." "A fist." "A hand." "We leapt like acrobats." Next time Ah Goong flattened himself on the ground, and the explosion rolled over him. . . .

The dynamite added more accidents and ways of dying, but if it were not used, the railroad would take fifty more years to finish. Nitroglycerine exploded when it was jounced on a horse or dropped. A man who fell with it in his pocket blew himself up into red pieces. Sometimes it combusted merely standing. Human bodies skipped through the air like puppets and made Ah Goong laugh crazily as if the arms and legs would come together again. The smell of burned flesh remained in rocks. . . .

Death in Winter

One day he came out of the tunnel to find the mountains white, the evergreens and bare trees decorated, white tree sculptures and lace bushes everywhere. The men from snow country called the icicles "ice chopsticks." He sat in his basket and slid down the slopes. The snow covered the gouged land, the broken trees, the tracks, the mud, the campfire ashes, the unburied dead. Streams were stilled in mid-run, the water petrified. That winter he thought it was the task of the human race to quicken the world, blast the freeze, fire it, redden it with blood. He had to change the stupid slowness of one sunrise and one sunset per day. He had to enliven the silent world with sound. "The rock," he tried to tell the others. "The ice." "Time."

The dynamiting loosed blizzards on the men. Ears and toes fell off. Fingers stuck to the cold silver rails. Snow-blind men stumbled about with bandannas over their eyes. Ah Goong helped build wood tunnels roofing the track route. Falling ice scrabbled on the roofs. The men stayed under the snow for weeks at a time. Snowslides covered the entrances to the tunnels, which they had to dig out to enter and exit, white tunnels and black tunnels. Ah Goong looked at his gang and thought, If there is an avalanche, these are the people I'll be trapped with, and wondered which ones would share food. . . .

The men who died slowly enough to say last words said, "Don't leave me frozen under the snow. Send my body home. Burn it and put the ashes in a tin can. Take the bone jar when you come down the mountain." "When you ride the fire car back to China, tell my descendants to come for me." "Shut up," scolded the hearty men. "We don't want to hear about bone jars and dying." "You're lucky to have a body to bury, not blown to smithereens." "Stupid man to hurt yourself," they bawled out the sick and wounded. How their wives would scold if they brought back deadmen's bones. "Aiya. To be buried here, nowhere." "But this is somewhere," Ah Goong promised. "This is the Gold Mountain. We're marking the land now. The track sections are numbered, and your family will know where we leave you." But he was a crazy man, and they didn't listen to him.

Spring did come, and when the snow melted, it revealed the past year, what had happened, what they had done, where they had worked, the lost tools, the thawing bodies, some standing with tools in hand, the bright rails. "Remember Uncle Long Winded Leong?" "Remember Strong Back Wong?" "Remember Lee Brother?" "And Fong Uncle?" They lost count of the number dead; there is no record of how many died building the railroad. Or maybe it was demons doing the counting and Chinamen not worth counting. Whether it was good luck or bad luck, the dead were hurled or cairned next to the last section of track they had worked on. "May his ghost not have to toil," they said over graves. (In China a woodcutter ghost chops eternally; people have heard chopping in the snow and in the heat. "Maybe his ghost will ride the train home." . . .

The Railroad Is Completed

There were two days that Ah Goong [cheered and threw] his hat in the air, jumping up and down and screaming Yippee like a cowboy. One: the day his team broke through the tunnel at last. Toward the end they did not dynamite but again used picks and sledge-hammers. Through the granite, they heard answering poundings, and answers to their shouts. It was not a mountain before them any more but only a wall with people breaking through from the other side. They worked faster. Forward. Into day. They stuck their arms through the holes and shook hands with men on the other side. Ah Goong saw dirty faces as wondrous as if he were seeing Nu Wo, the creator goddess who repairs cracks in the sky with stone slabs; sometimes she peeks through and human beings see her face. The wall broke. Each team gave the other a gift of half a tunnel, dug. They stepped back and forth where the wall had been. Ah Goong ran and ran, his boots thudding to the very end of the tunnel, looked at the other side of the mountain, and ran back, clear through the entire tunnel. All the way through.

He spent the rest of his time on the railroad laying and bending and hammering the ties and rails. The second day the Chinamen cheered was when the engine from the West and the one from the East rolled toward one another and touched. The transcontinental railroad was finished. They Yippee'd like madmen. The white demon officials gave speeches. "The Greatest Feat of the Nineteenth Century," they said. "The Greatest Feat in the History of Mankind," they said. "Only Americans could have done it," they said, which is true. Even if Ah Goong had not spent half his gold on Citizenship Papers, he was an American for having built the railroad. A white demon in top hat tap-tapped on the gold spike, and pulled it back out. Then one China Man held the real spike, the steel one, and another hammered it in.

Sold into Slavery

Ruthanne Lum McCunn

Most Chinese immigrants coming to America were men who came willingly. In this excerpt from *Thousand Pieces of Gold*, Ruthanne Lum McCunn provides a fictionalized account of the life of a real Chinese girl who came to the United States unwillingly. McCunn describes the experience of Lalu Nathoy, a teenage peasant girl who became a slave when her father was forced to sell her for two bags of grain during a famine in northern China. Lalu was taken to Shanghai, where she was sold again and put on a ship to America with other young slave women. Not understanding she was still to be a slave, she was then put on the auction block in San Francisco, an event described by McCunn in this selection, and sold to a Chinese immigrant saloonkeeper.

Lalu was eventually transported to her new owner's Idaho mining town, given the name "Polly," and forced to work without pay in the saloon. "Polly" eventually married another saloonkeeper, Charlie Bemis, who had won her in a card game, and she lived the rest of her life in Idaho. Lalu Polly Bemis died in 1933. McCunn is an American of Scottish and Chinese ancestry who has won several prizes for her books on the Chinese experience in America.

"Those with contracts come over to this side, those without go stand on the platform," an old woman in black lacquer pants and jacket directed.

Lalu held out her papers. The old woman took them. She pushed Lalu in the direction of the women without contracts.

"No, I belong over there," Lalu said, trying to take back the papers.

The old woman snorted. "What a bumpkin you are! Those papers were just to get you into the country. They have to be used again."

"But Li Ma said . . ."

"Don't argue girl, you're one of the lucky ones," the old woman said. She pointed to the group of women with contracts. "Their fates have been decided, it's prostitution for them, but if you play your cards right, you may still get the bridal chair."

Shock Runs Through the Crowd

A shocked murmur rippled through the group of women. One of them took a paper from an inner pocket. "I have a marriage contract," she said. "Not what you suggest."

"And I! And I!" the women around her echoed.

The old woman took the contract from the young woman. The paper crackled as she spread it open. "Read it!" she ordered.

The young woman's lips quivered. "I can't."

The old woman jangled the ring of keys at her waist. "Does anyone here read?"

The women looked hopefully at each other. Some shook their heads. Others were simply silent. None could read.

"Then I'll tell you what your contracts say." Without looking at any of the papers, the old woman continued, "For the sum of your passage money, you have promised the use of your bodies for prostitution."

"But the marriage broker gave my parents the passage money," the young woman persisted.

"You fool, that was a procurer, not a marriage broker!" She pointed to the thumb print at the bottom of the paper. "Is that your mark?"

Sobbing quietly, the young woman nodded.

"Well then, there's nothing more to be said, is there?"

"Yes there is," a girl said boldly. "I put my mark on one

of those contracts, and I knew what it was for." Her face reddened. "I had to," she added.

"So?" the old woman, hands on hips, prompted.

"The contract specifies the number of years, five in my case, so take heart sisters, our shame will not last forever."

"What about your sick days?"

"What do you mean?" the girl asked.

"The contract states your monthly sick days will be counted against your time: two weeks for one sick day, another month for each additional sick day."

Never to Be Free

"But that means I'll never be free!"

"Exactly."

Like a stone dropped in a pond, the word started wave after wave of talk and tears.

"Keep crying like that," the old woman shouted, "and by the time your owners come to get you, your eyes will be swollen like toads."

"What difference does it make?" a voice challenged.

"Depending on your looks, you can be placed in an elegant house and dressed in silks and jewels or in a bagnio."

"Bagnio?"

"On your way here you must have seen the doors with the barred windows facing the alleys, but perhaps you did not hear the chickens inside, tapping and scratching the screens, trying to attract a man without bringing a cop. Cry, make yourself ugly, and you'll be one of those chickens, charging twenty-five cents for a look, fifty cents for a feel, and seventy-five cents for action."

Slowly the sobs became muted sniffles and whimpers as stronger women hushed the weaker. The old woman turned to Lalu's group. "Now get up on that platform like I told you."

Silently Lalu and the other women and girls obeyed.

When they were all on the platform, the old woman began to speak.

"This is where you'll stand tomorrow when the men come. There'll be merchants, miners, well-to-do peddlers, brothel owners, and those who just want to look. They'll examine you for soundness and beauty. Do yourself up right, smile sweetly, and the bids will come in thick and fast from those looking for wives as well as those looking to fill a house.

"When the price is agreed on, the buyer will place the money in your hands. That will make the sale binding, but you will turn the money over to me. Do you understand?"

The women and girls nodded. A few murmured defeat.

The old woman pointed to some buckets against the wall. "There's soap and water. Wash thoroughly. You will be stripped for auction."

"Stripped?"

"Women in the Gold Mountains are scarcer than hen's teeth and even a plain or ugly girl has value. But when a man has to pay several thousand dollars for a woman, he likes to see exactly what he is buying," the old woman said.

Scarcer than Hen's Teeth

She grabbed a tight-lipped, thin, dark girl from the back of the group. The girl stared defiant as the old woman ripped off her jacket and pointed out scars from a deep hatchet wound, puckered flesh the shape of a hot iron. "Look carefully and be warned against any thought of disobedience or escape." She threw the girl's jacket onto the floor. "It will be the bagnio for you. If you're lucky."

She pulled the women closest to her down from the platform and herded them toward the buckets of water. "Now get going, we've wasted time enough."

All around her, Lalu could hear the sounds of women and girls preparing themselves for auction, but she made no move to join them. It had taken all her concentration to make out the words that had been spoken in the strange Southern dialect, and she was only just beginning to feel their impact.

She had been duped, she realized. By the soft voiced, gentle Madam, a cormorant who had nothing to give except to its master.[1] By Li Ma, the foulmouthed procuress charged with Lalu's delivery to the auction room. By the talk of freemen whose dreams could never be hers. For the Gold Mountains they had described was not the America she would know. This: the dingy basement room, the blank faces of women and girls stripped of hope, the splintered boards beneath her feet, the auction block. This was her America.

---

1. Chinese fishermen used cormorants to catch fish by tying a rope around their legs. When they had caught a fish, the fishermen made them regurgitate it.

Racism and Anti-Chinese Legislation

Stanford M. Lyman

Stanford M. Lyman recounts examples of prejudice against Chinese immigrants in this passage from his book Chinese Americans. *Lyman points out that as the Chinese immigrant population in America grew in the second half of the nineteenth century, an anti-Chinese movement grew with it. Numerous incidents of brutal violence were perpetrated against innocent Chinese workers during this period. In addition, legislation was passed to control or harass Chinese workers. The most significant legislation was the federal Chinese Exclusion Act of 1882, which banned further immigration of all Chinese laborers. Other legislation restricted the occupations that Chinese could enter and forced some Chinese workers from their jobs. Punitive legislation also was common, such as the "cubic air law," which discriminated against Chinese who had been forced by poverty to live in crowded, ghettolike conditions in San Francisco. Lyman is a professor at the New School for Social Research in New York and the author of many books on sociological topics, including* The Asian in North America.

The Chinese were objects of racist thought even before they arrived in America. American interest in China dated from the colonial commerce with Canton. The China trade enriched New England merchants and shippers in the late eighteenth century and encouraged them to seek to wrest this lucrative business from British domination. But an interest in Chinese material culture—chinoiserie, tea, architecture, and gardens—was not matched by a sympathy for Chinese people. Until the outbreak of the opium wars (1839), American traders in China reported that the Chinese were "ridiculously clad, superstitious ridden, dishonest, crafty, cruel, and marginal members of the human race who lacked the courage, intelligence, skill, and will to do anything about the oppressive despotism under which they lived or the stagnating social conditions that surrounded them," [according to Stuart Creighton Miller].

Although trader prejudices were limited for the most part to commentaries arising out of experiences with Chinese merchants, officials, and servants, American Protestant missionaries, ruled by passion for their divine mission, tended to impugn the morality of the whole Chinese nation. To missionaries bent on conversion the ordinary Chinese were debased heathens awaiting divine rescue from their unholy condition of "lechery, dishonesty, xenophobia, cruelty, despotism, filth, and intellectual inferiority," [writes Miller]. Diplomats and intellectuals added a body of racist writings to the traders' gratuitous insults and the missionaries' self-righteous outrage. American officials and intellectuals in China combined a principled attack on Chinese political institutions with an ethnocentric account of Chinese culture and a moralistic indictment of the entire society. . . .

Chinese immigration to California from 1848 to 1882 occasioned a great national and cultural debate. The doctrines of white supremacy and Anglo-conformity, which had already dispensed with full citizenship for the Negro and the Indian and suffered European immigration only with considerable distrust and suspicion, took on an even sharper racial and cultural edge. New anxieties were aroused by the Chinese presence: they would give impetus to the dying institution of slavery, introduce still another race incompatible with the dominant Caucasian stock, and spread new and incurable sicknesses. As reports of poverty, filth, disease, and cruelty emanated from strife-torn China, the Chinese immigrants were tarred with the Sinophobic brush. The new polygenetic theory of the origin of races stamped anti-Chinese attitudes with the authority of science, the enunciation of the germ theory of culture encouraged nonassimilation, and the newly aroused interest in public health stimulated worry about the threat of exotic and loathsome diseases alleged to be peculiar to the Chinese. American leaders, still doubtful about the triumph of white civilization in America, focused their attention increasingly on "the Chinese question." In 1882 Senator Saulsburg of Delaware probably summed up the opinion of many Americans about the Chinese when he declared, "They are of a different race and possess an entirely different civilization, and in my opinion are incapable of being brought into assimilation in habits, customs, and manners with the people of this country."

The Anti-Chinese Movement, 1852–1910

Although a national feeling against the Chinese had been aroused even before the first immigrant debarked at San Francisco, it was their presence in the California mines and in other primary laboring occupations and the prediction that they would "swarm" over the whole nation that triggered repressive action.

At first only the Chinese miner encountered hostility because of the allegation that he was robbing the state of its mineral wealth and shipping gold to China. The gold mines of California and the other western states were never in fact dominated by the Chinese. Indeed, Chinese mineworkers often confined their labors to claims already abandoned by whites. Nevertheless, they were attacked vigorously and viciously for more than thirty years by both public laws and popular uprisings.

While California's miners complained about unfair Chinese competition, entrepreneurs sought to exploit the Chinese worker. In 1852 California State Senator George B. Tingley introduced a bill to legalize contract labor for periods of ten years or less. In an attack on this "coolie bill," Senator Philip Roach, who was to become a lifelong opponent of Chinese immigration, indicated that opposition to the enserfment of Chinese laborers was not motivated by human compassion or by an egalitarian interest in workingmen. "We are called upon," he declared, "to enact a law by which the surplus and inferior population of Asia may be brought into competition with the labor of our own people.". . .

Chinese, according to Roach's conception, were to be treated like Negroes and Indians: denied citizenship and a chance to compete in the world of industrial labor, they might be mudsills [persons of low social class]. Roach emphasized his demand for exclusion of Chinese from the skilled occupations: "I do not want to see Chinese or Kanaka [native Hawaiian] carpenters, masons, or blacksmiths, brought here in swarms under contracts, to compete with our own mechanics whose labor is as honorable and as well entitled to social and political rights as the pursuits designated 'learned professions.'"

Violence Against Chinese

Even before the infamous suggestion that contract labor be legalized in California, the Chinese miners were subjected to popular tribunals and mob violence. In the town of Chinese Camp as early as 1849 an uprising against sixty Chinese began what was to become more than a half-century of violence. The debate over the "coolie bill" sparked local movements to expel the Chinese from mining areas throughout California. At Columbia, Tuolomne County, on May 8, 1852, white miners drew up a resolution excluding all Asiatics from the mines and appointing a

Vigilance Committee to enforce its decision. At Marysville another miners' assembly declared that "no Chinaman was to be thenceforth allowed to hold any mining claim in the neighborhood." A movement to expel Chinese from the area gained widespread support. Accompanied by a marching band and a carnival atmosphere, white miner groups drove the Chinese from North Forks, Horseshoe Bar, and other neighboring camps. . . .

Chinese miners, workers, and laundrymen were the principal victims of the working-class nativism that spread over the Rocky Mountains region in the latter quarter of the nineteenth century. The Idaho Territory proved to be a particularly harsh place for Chinese. For example, in 1885 a merchant in Pierce was murdered, and five Chinese, accused of the crime, were hanged by a mob. After an official complaint from the Chinese government and an inquiry from the Secretary of State, the territorial government determined to rid the area of Chinese. A committee of women from Helena, Montana, "welcomed" the Chinese to the city by giving them notice that they must at once "suspend the washing or laundry business." A few years later Montana required all hand laundries to be licensed at a fee of $10 per quarter on pain of a jail sentence of six months or a fine of not more than $500 or both. Chinese in Tonapah, Nevada, were summarily ordered out of town by a committee of white men; when they begged for time to gather their possessions, they were set upon, robbed, and beaten, sustaining one death. Chinese railway workers and hawkers were also driven away by mobs of unionized white workers in Virginia City and Gold Hill.

The Anti-Chinese Movement that had begun in the mines of California spread to the Midwest and, as Chinese laborers reached the eastern cities of the United States, engulfed the nation. The objections to the Chinese were broad and vague, derived from the half-century of vilification by traders, missionaries, and diplomats, but enhanced by the outraged cries of racist union leaders, small-scale farmers, and exploitative businessmen. In general, Chinese immigrants were held to be servile as laborers, unfair in their competition with white workingmen, vicious in their ethics, immoral in their conduct, contagious and disease ridden, and subject to a private government outside the control of American law. In addition, the fact that they sent much of their earnings to China and that they were regarded as an unassimilable people, aroused concern, indignation, and contempt.

Anti-Chinese Legislation

The attacks on the Chinese were not confined to uprisings in the mines, assaults on railway workers, or urban riots. Indeed it would be misleading to suppose that antagonism toward the Chinese arose solely because of the frustrations of white workingmen or depredations by fanatical, sick, or savage individuals. Hostility to the Chinese became a political platform on which hundreds of campaigns for public office were launched. Leaders of labor unions defined the "Chinese question" as the central political issue of the day. Business interests perceived the Chinese as an exploitable element in the labor force who, although they ought not to be absolutely excluded, nevertheless should be prevented from assuming full citizenship or social equality. Missionaries defended Chinese from the most severe of Sinophobic outrages, but they deserted the field when conversions proved too few to justify their endeavor. In short, there were no elites who favored the Chinese. Scorned by officials, patronized by missionaries, defamed by labor leaders, and battered by mobs, the Chinese suffered nearly the full panoply of injustice that a racist society could impose.

Anti-Chinese legislation was of three kinds. The first

consisted of state and ultimately federal laws to restrict or exclude Chinese from immigrating to America. The second sought to eliminate Chinese from occupations in which they allegedly competed unfairly with white labor. Finally, a number of laws had either a punitive or harassing intent. . . .

Immigration Legislation

Pressures on Congress and the President resulted in a renegotiation of the Burlingame Treaty—which, among other things, had recognized the inalienable right of people to cross national boundaries and change their place of habitat—to permit "the Government of the United States [to] regulate, limit, or suspend such coming and residence, but . . . not absolutely prohibit it." Congress quickly passed a measure to suspend the immigration of Chinese laborers for seventy years, but President Rutherford Hayes vetoed it. A subsequent measure, reducing the suspension period to ten years, was signed by President Hayes and became law on May 6, 1882.

The Chinese exclusion act provided that no skilled or unskilled Chinese laborer or miner could enter the United States for ten years, but it exempted certified merchants, students, and itinerants from this prohibition. The law contained so many confusing, complex, and ambiguous clauses and requirements that its effect was to promote both evasion by the Chinese and unusually harsh treatment of legitimate arrivals by immigration inspectors. Subsequent amendments to the act obviated certain confusions and inequities but served to create new ones. The Chinese government sought modification of the harsher features of the exclusion act in the proposed Sino-American Treaty of 1888. However, during the debates occasioned by the treaty, rumors of China's resistance were spread, and the impending presidential election colored congressional discussion. In response to a newspaper report that China had rejected the treaty, Congress passed the Scott Act, which provided that any Chinese who had not returned to the United States before the law's passage was to be refused admission; that no more certificates of identity and readmission, required under the original exclusion law, should be issued; and that all outstanding certificates were null and void. The Scott Act survived Supreme Court scrutiny even though it clearly went beyond the stipulations of the Treaty of 1880. China protested in vain for four years, but its official notes went unanswered.

The stringent regulation of Chinese immigration continued during the next decade. The Fifty-Second Congress disposed of twelve different bills for the regulation of Chinese immigration. At length the unusually harsh Geary Act became law (May 5, 1892). Not only did this piece of legislation extend all existing laws restricting Chinese immigration for another decade, but it also placed the burden of proving their right to be in the United States on the Chinese immigrants. In addition, the Geary Act denied bail to Chinese in habeas corpus proceedings, prescribed a prison sentence of one year for all violators, and ordered deportation to the country to which the illegal resident was subject upon completion of his or her term of imprisonment. The most onerous provision of the new law was its requirement that all Chinese laborers carry certificates of residence. Similar to certification procedures required of free Negroes and itinerant slaves in the antebellum South and to those in force in Czarist Russia and much later under South Africa's system of apartheid, the American certification regulation required that all Chinese laborers living in the United States apply for a certificate of residence. Certification required a complete registration of identification for each applicant. Enforcement was placed in the hands of the Collector of Internal Revenue, with whom a duplicate certificate was filed. . . .

Occupational Restrictions

A major source of anti-Chinese sentiment in America after 1850 was organized labor. Composed largely of European immigrants and white American workingmen, the unions attached racial animosity toward Chinese—and later toward Negroes, Japanese, Indians, and Mexicans—to their economic program of labor reform. With the rare and innocuous exception of the International Workers of the World and a few isolated voices within the ranks of the more moderate workingmen's associations, labor was unanimous in its insistence that Chinese immigrants degraded white labor, reduced wages, encouraged exploitation, and were culturally and morally inferior. Moreover, it was the leadership of the labor movement that provided the most outrageous rhetoric, vicious accusations, and pejorative demagoguery for the American Sinophobic movement.

Having significant influence in the molding of American public opinion and in some states a powerful voice in shaping public policy, labor's hostility to the Chinese did much to translate the Sinophobic sentiment in America into hardened law. Beginning with local restrictions on Chinese laborers in rural mining areas the organized workingman's movement mounted a racist campaign against the Chinese in the cities. Anticoolie clubs sprang up throughout the West, and similar associations were sponsored in the eastern cities of the United States after Chinese laborers had been imported in order to break strikes in Boston, Cleveland, and Passaic, New Jersey. Moreover, these clubs were the springboard for agitators who organized mobs that attacked and burned Chinese business operations and beat and murdered Asian workers during moments of great economic crisis. . . .

Labor carried out a campaign of occupational eviction against the Chinese which culminated in their nearly complete disappearance from the labor market by 1910. In that year no Chinese whatsoever was reported working in the metalliferous mines of Colorado, Montana, Arizona, or California. The smelting and refining industries in Colorado and Montana not only had eliminated the Chinese but also, by means of a literacy and citizenship test, had removed Japanese, Italians, Negroes, and Greeks as well. Although Chinese constituted the exclusive labor force of Wyoming's coal mines after 1869, they were forcibly removed from their positions by a series of riots and strikes after 1882.

The worst of these was the infamous riot at Rock Springs, Wyoming, on September 2, 1885. Set off over an argument between a Chinese and white employee about work in the mineshafts, the violence resulted in the deaths of twenty-eight Chinese, the wounding of fifteen others, and the forcible expulsion of the remaining Chinese from the community. After two years of acrimonious bickering the United States Government agreed to pay an indemnification of $147,748.74 to the Chinese government to compensate the survivors for the losses sustained. By 1940 only fifty-five Chinese remained in the vicinity of Rock Springs, a town that in 1890 had complained of the presence of nearly 500. . . .

Labor's campaign against Chinese workers in the city had a significant result: Chinese, forced out of their jobs in factories and industries located throughout the city, retired to Chinatown, becoming part of its isolated, overworked, and underpaid labor force. Where this did not happen, as in the gunpowder factories of San Francisco, Chinese laborers were employed in segregated gangs in the most dangerous aspect of the work, the handling of black powder. Although Chinese were regarded as the most efficient workingmen in their department, they were paid a lower wage than white workers and offered a much lower indemnity in case of death through industrial accident. . . .

Harassing Legislation

A few of the laws enacted during the height of the Anti-Chinese Movement had little purpose other than to harass, annoy, and humiliate the hapless Asian sojourners. Among the most significant of these laws were the ordinances covering lodging houses, cutting hair, delivering goods, and disinterring the dead.

The ordinance regulating lodging houses was passed on July 29, 1870, but not enforced until three years later. It required that every house or room occupied as a lodging should contain within the walls at least 500 cubic feet of air space for each adult who resided therein. In 1873, in the wake of widespread urban unemployment and fierce hostility toward the Chinese, San Francisco began arresting Chinese for violation of the "cubic air" law, as it came to be called. Chinese prisoners refused to pay bail or fines and filled the jails. Their protest embarrassed city officials because, although the law did not apply to prisons, the overcrowded jails clearly afforded each Chinese prisoner less than 100 cubic feet of air space. In September 1873 the lodging house ordinance was declared void by the county court.

In retaliation against the Chinese refusal to pay bail or fines, the Board of Supervisors passed the "queue" ordinance, requiring that "each and every male prisoner incarcerated or imprisoned in the county jail . . . shall . . . have the hair of their head cut or clipped to a uniform length of one inch from the scalp thereof"; a "laundry" ordinance which required $15 per quarter license fee for all laundries using no horse-drawn vehicles, with lesser fees for those employing horses; and a third ordinance that required a coroner's written permission to remove bodies from any cemetery or graveyard, with violators subject to a penalty of not less than $100 or more than $500. The Chinese braid or queue was the badge of citizenship required by the Manchu government for all its subjects; its loss would place any Chinese in serious civil jeopardy. It was well known that Chinese laundrymen did not use horse-drawn wagons; their special mode of delivery, walking with poles across their shoulders on the ends of which they suspended goods, had already been prohibited by a law of 1870. The cemetery laws sought to harass the Chinese who wished to follow the traditional practice of burying the dead in the village from which they had come. . . .

Objectives Reached

The Anti-Chinese Movement achieved its main objectives by 1910. By that year the trade unions succeeded in eliminating Chinese workers from the labor market; legislative restriction, combining an exclusion of Chinese laborers and their wives with a prohibition on naturalization, promised an eventual elimination of the Chinese population in the United States; the shortage of women among the Chinese seemed to indicate that no large number of American citizens of Chinese extraction would be born in the United States; and the merchant elite of Chinatown apparently assumed an almost extraterritorial sovereignty and a benevolent but despotic protection over the dispossessed, alien, and aging Chinese sojourners.

"The Chinese Invasion": A Threat to American Workers

Dennis Kearney and H.L. Knight

Many workingmen lost their jobs when the United States entered a period of economic depression in the 1870s. In this era of social and economic upheaval, people sought someone to blame, and all too often Chinese immigrants became scapegoats. In this selection originally published in the *Indianapolis Times* in 1878, Dennis Kearney, president of California's Workingman's Party, and H.L. Knight, party secretary, explain their view of the threat that the Chinese posed to American workers. Kearney and Knight advocate the forcible expulsion of Chinese workers from the United States. They blame workers' problems on cheap Chinese labor and on the greed and mismanagement of capitalists. They also describe the Chinese laborers as living like serfs and slaves, thus undercutting the ability of American workers to find jobs with livable wages. Kearney regularly roused crowds of white unemployed workers with fiery harangues that typically ended with the words, "The Chinese must go!"

Our moneyed men have ruled us for the past thirty years. Under the flag of the slaveholder they hoped to destroy our liberty. Failing in that, they have rallied under the banner of the millionaire, the banker and the land monopo-

Dennis Kearney and H.L. Knight, "Appeal from California. The Chinese Invasion. Workingmen's Address," *Indianapolis Times*, February 28, 1878.

list, the railroad king and the false politician, to effect their purpose.

The Threat of the Moneyed Class

We have permitted them to become immensely rich against all sound republican policy, and they have turned upon us to sting us to death. They have seized upon the government by bribery and corruption. They have made speculation and public robbery a science. They have loaded the nation, the state, the county, and the city with debt. They have stolen the public lands. They have grasped all to themselves, and by their unprincipled greed brought a crisis of unparalleled distress on forty millions of people, who have natural resources to feed, clothe and shelter the whole human race.

Such misgovernment, such mismanagement, may challenge the whole world for intense stupidity, and would put to shame the darkest tyranny of the barbarous past.

We, here in California, feel it as well as you. We feel that the day and hour has come for the Workingmen of America to depose capital and put Labor in the Presidential chair, in the Senate and Congress, in the State House, and on the Judicial Bench. We are with you in this work. Workingmen must form a party of their own, take charge of the government, dispose gilded fraud, and put honest toil in power.

In our golden state all these evils have been intensified. Land monopoly has seized upon all the best soil in this fair land. A few men own from ten thousand to two hundred thousand acres each. The poor Laborer can find no resting place, save on the barren mountain, or in the trackless desert. Money monopoly has reached its grandest proportions. Here, in San Francisco, the palace of the millionaire looms up above the hovel of the starving poor with as wide a contrast as anywhere on earth.

The Threat of Cheap Chinese Labor

To add to our misery and despair, a bloated aristocracy has sent to China—the greatest and oldest despotism in the world—for a cheap working slave. It rakes the slums of Asia to find the meanest slave on earth—the Chinese coolie—and imports him here to meet the free American in the Labor market, and still further widen the breach between the rich and the poor, still further to degrade white Labor.

These cheap slaves fill every place. Their dress is scant and cheap. Their food is rice from China. They hedge twenty in a room, ten by ten. They are whipped curs, abject in docility, mean, contemptible and obedient in all things. They have no wives, children or dependents.

They are imported by companies, controlled as serfs, worked like slaves, and at last go back to China with all their earnings. They are in every place, they seem to have no sex. Boys work, girls work; it is all alike to them.

The father of a family is met by them at every turn. Would he get work for himself? Ah! A stout Chinaman does it cheaper. Will he get a place for his oldest boy? He can not. His girl? Why, the Chinaman is in her place too! Every door is closed. He can only go to crime or suicide, his wife and daughter to prostitution, and his boys to hoodlumism and the penitentiary.

A Call for Defiance

Do not believe those who call us savages, rioters, incendiaries, and outlaws. We seek our ends calmly, rationally, at the ballot box. So far good order has marked all our proceedings. But, we know how false, how inhuman, our adversaries are. We know that if gold, if fraud, if force can defeat us, they will all be used. And we have resolved that they shall not defeat us. We shall arm. We shall meet fraud and falsehood with defiance, and force with force, if need be.

We are men, and propose to live like men in this free

land, without the contamination of slave labor, or die like men, if need be, in asserting the rights of our race, our country, and our families.

California must be all American or all Chinese. We are resolved that it shall be American, and are prepared to make it so. May we not rely upon your sympathy and assistance?

With great respect for the Workingman's Party of California,

Dennis Kearney, President

H.L. Knight, Secretary

CHAPTER 2

Early Struggles and Achievements from the First Wave to World War II

COMING TO AMERICA

Eyewitness to an Anti-Chinese Riot

Him Mark Lai

Chinese laborers were denied entry into the United States after 1882. Despite the subsequent decline in the Chinese population, anti-Chinese sentiment persisted well into the twentieth century. Violent incidents, including hundreds of murders, occurred frequently in the American West during this period. In this selection author Him Mark Lai translates the text of a letter sent by Chinese residents of Tonopah, Nevada, to the Chinese Consolidated Benevolent Association in San Francisco. The Chinese residents of Tonopah describe an anti-Chinese riot that occurred on November 15, 1903; the riot resulted in the murder of one immigrant. The Chinese sought legal remedy for the assault, but in the court case that followed, all the white rioters were found not guilty. The Chinese residents were denied indemnity payments for the assaults and property damage. Him Mark Lai is a professor at San Francisco State University and the author of several works about Chinese immigrants.

In order to report in detail our forced expulsion from the town of Tonopah by a vicious gang of Labor Union members on the evening of the 25th day of the 7th moon [September 15, 1903], we beg the editors of the eminent newspaper *Chung Sai Yat Po* to take the trouble to publish this in the newspaper to spread the news far and near so that

Him Mark Lai, "The 1903 Anti-Chinese Riot in Tonopah, Nevada, from a Chinese Perspective: Two Letters Published in the *Chung Sai Yat Po*," *Chinese America: History and Perspectives*, 2003, p. 47. Copyright © 2003 by the Chinese Historical Society of America. Reproduced by permission.

our fellow countrymen will all know about the tragic events that occurred in our community. We will be extremely grateful for your favor. . . .

A fellow countryman [Chinese] rented a place for $100 per month and opened on Monday, the 24th day of the 7th moon, or September 14 [1903]. Who would have guessed that that Labor Union[1] would again immediately create a furor? They held a meeting at 8:00 P.M. on the 15th. The Labor Union leader, by the name of Arandall, whom the group addressed as President, had opened a clothing market during the winter of the 27th year [1901–02]. His workmanship was not skillful and his prices high, and the Westerners did not think highly of him. He had harbored his resentment for a long time; therefore he used this opportunity as a pretext and declared to the members: "The Chinese presence today is detrimental to our Union. Since we are now strong, it would be better and timely to expel them completely to avoid future problems. What do you think?" The crowd signaled their approval of his proposal. Between 8:00 and 9:00 P.M. on the evening of the 25th day of the 7th moon [September 15], sixty to seventy members gathered and descended on Chinatown and laundries like a swarm of bees to expel the Chinese, demanding that they leave town immediately or else be killed without exception.

At that time a fellow countryman reasoned with them and said, "If you want us to leave, we will leave, but we cannot leave so quickly. If you give us a time limit, we will surely leave as you wish." But those ruffians would not accept any explanations and immediately seized our throats with both hands, intending to kill us. Fortunately, there were among them some good-hearted individuals, who counseled them to release us and then set a 24-hour limit within which all Chinese would have to leave town. If they

1. a local group of cooks, waiters, dishwashers, and woodcutters who named themselves the "Labor Union"

had not left by the time limit, they would all be hung or killed without exception.

The group also went to other places, harassing residences one after another. This was the first time these places had been visited, and actually nobody was harmed nor property damaged. The individuals can only say that they were bullied, and we also thought that it would only come to that. Our fellow countrymen prepared to leave town at daybreak and then report the incident to the authorities. By this time Li Maofen [Charlie Fawn] of Heshan had already gone looking for the constable to ask for protection. Who could have known that the officers of the court and their staff all belonged to that gang? All had gone into hiding beforehand. When Li Maofen finally found the constable, the latter made excuses and ignored his request. Since Li's laundry was at the edge of town and he was fearful that the vicious ruffians would return, he begged the constable to put him in the jail to keep him alive that night, whereupon the constable led Li to the jail to stay for the night.

When this happened, it was only about 10:00 P.M. If the constable knew that he would be unable to protect the Chinese, why didn't he ring the bell to sound the alarm? Instead, he waited until daybreak before he spoke to others, and still pretended that he did not know what had happened. But after the ruffians had expelled all of us, they returned to the bar to drink and make merry and shout that all the pigtailed Chinese had been chased out of town. How could he not hear and know about this? That is why we say that the town constable actually intended to let the ruffians have their way. Even if he gives a hundred excuses, he cannot be absolved of blame. When Li Maofen found him, it was only about 10:00 P.M. Why didn't he find means to provide protection? If he had done so, the later rash of injuries by beating would not have occurred. Moreover, earlier, under the pretext of searching for opium, that constable had gone through houses and rooms, overturning chests and ransacking suitcases, and exposing all the money and goods. This was illegal; however, we had no choice but to let him do as he wished.

A Vicious Attack

Who was to know that at 11:00 P.M. or 12:00 midnight that night, members of the Labor Union would gather and descend on us like a swarm of bees, with each person bearing firearms? Their ferocity and cruelty exceeded that of wild animals. They broke down doors to gain entry and pistol-whipped people they encountered right and left, destroyed furnishings and goods, and searched for and seized money. Afterward they herded the Chinese out of town under guard, some for 2 to 3 miles, others for 4 to 5 miles, and then fired several pistol shots. Fortunately, no one was hurt. However, the guards were beating the Chinese as they were on the way out of town, so a number sustained head injuries. Among those forced to leave town, eight were severely wounded. . . . Some were injured even while they were proceeding under guard within the town limits. Several residences were wrecked and countless furnishings damaged.

After the incident and [after] the Chinese returned to town and accounted for the people [who had been herded out of town], it was discovered that Zhang Bingliang [a laundry owner] was missing. On the morning of the 26th day of the 7th moon [September 16], we sent telegrams to the Chinese Consolidated Benevolent Association and the Chinese Consulate General [in San Francisco] asking them to find means to provide protection. Your Excellency the consul then sent a telegram to the [Chinese] envoy [in Washington, D.C.]. The latter immediately dispatched a telegram to the Nevada State governor, who in turn telegraphed the town, ordering the merchant leaders to do their utmost to provide protection.

Even before receipt of this telegram, some business leaders had come to Chinatown to advise our fellow countrymen: "Do not be afraid and leave town. We merchant leaders surely will work out a plan to provide protection." Later that evening, after receiving the telegram from the governor at Carson City, they called a special meeting to discuss how to exert every effort to provide protection. We saw that they were sincere and therefore felt somewhat more at ease. We also met and decided to send people in different directions to look for Uncle Zhang Bingliang. They all returned by nightfall and reported that they could not find him. The next morning everybody again went searching in different directions, bringing along tea, rations, and herbs. Westerners and Indians also joined the search. A little after 10:00 A.M., a Westerner found Uncle Zhang Bingliang dead by the roadside about 3 miles out of town. The Westerner returned to town to report his find. The government attorney ordered the corpse returned in a wagon [and that it] be examined for the record, and we then reclaimed the body to be buried with appropriate rites.

The injuries on Uncle Zhang Bingliang were horrible. According to the doctor's examination, he was injured by a chopping hatchet blow on his forehead, his back was black and blue, and his entire body was covered with wounds. All men and women looking on who had any compassion at all could not help but weep. On that same day, based on evidence provided by Chinese and Westerner witnesses, seventeen ruffians were jailed. However, the ruffians were wicked and had ample financial resources. They hired six lawyers, intending to exert every effort to win this case.

The Poetry of Angel Island

Anonymous Poets

During the first half of the twentieth century, would-be Chinese immigrants were detained on Angel Island in San Francisco Bay until applications for entry could be processed. The immigrants were often questioned very closely and were asked to prove their identities. The wait at the Angel Island detention center routinely stretched into weeks or months. To express their feelings about these circumstances Chinese immigrants wrote poetry on the walls of the detention center barracks. The poetry reflects the immigrants' hopes, fears, sadness, and sometimes fury at American immigration authorities. This selection of poetry was collected from the Angel Island detention center walls as part of a project sponsored by the Chinese Culture Foundation of San Francisco.

1.
Instead of remaining a citizen of China, I willingly
    became an ox.
I intended to come to America to earn a living.
The Western styled buildings are lofty; but I have not
    the luck to live in them.
How was anyone to know that my dwelling place would
    be a prison?
2.
The west wind ruffles my thin gauze clothing.

Him Mark Lai, Genny Lim, and Judy Yung, *Island: Poetry and History of Chinese Immigrants on Angel Island, 1910–1940*. San Francisco: HOC DOI, 1986.

On the hill sits a tall building with a room of wooden
planks.
I wish I could travel on a cloud far away, reunite with my
wife and son.
When the moonlight shines on me alone, the nights seem
even longer.
At the head of the bed there is wine and my heart is
constantly drunk.
There is no flower beneath my pillow and my dreams are
not sweet.
To whom can I confide my innermost feelings?
I rely solely on close friends to relieve my loneliness.
3.
America has power, but not justice.
In prison, we were victimized as if we were guilty.
Given no opportunity to explain, it was really brutal.
I bow my head in reflection but there is nothing I can do.
4.
This place is called an island of immortals,
When, in fact, this mountain wilderness is a prison.
Once you see the open net, why throw yourself in?
It is only because of empty pockets I can do nothing
else.
5.
Leaving behind my writing brush and removing my
sword, I came to America.
Who was to know two streams of tears would flow upon
arriving here?
If there comes a day when I will have attained my
ambition and become successful,
I will certainly behead the barbarians and spare not a
single blade of grass.

Entering America with Forged Papers

Tung Pok Chin, with Winifred C. Chin

When the Chinese Exclusion Act of 1882 denied legal entry to Chinese laborers, many Chinese immigrants looked for a way to circumvent this discriminatory law. Because U.S. law allowed a child of an American citizen to immigrate legally, many immigrants purchased forged documents on the black market to prove they qualified. Those who entered in this manner were called "paper sons." In this first-person account Tung Pok Chin, with the help of his daughter, Winifred C. Chin, describes how he became a paper son in 1934 and entered the United States at the age of nineteen. His father, a noncitizen resident of the United States, paid for the forged documents and passage to the United States. Chin worked for other Chinese immigrants, but eventually took over his father's laundry in Massachusetts. Chin describes the challenge of paying back the cost of forged papers at the low salaries most Chinese immigrants earned. Winifred C. Chin is associate professor of religious studies at St. Francis College in Brooklyn.

I arrived in the United States in Boston in 1934 at the age of nineteen. I had purchased my "paper," designating me the son of an American native, on the Chinese black market, and would automatically become a United States citizen upon verification of the facts. For months before leaving China I studied these "facts": my paper name, my paper father's name, my paper mother's name, my age, their ages, my place of birth, their places of birth, their occupations, and so on.

Immigration Interrogation

This was not easy. I had to completely block out my real and immediate family: my parents who raised me and arranged a marriage for me at the age of thirteen, my wife, my two young sons, aged four and five at the time of my arrival in Boston, and all else that related to them. One slip during the interrogation and I would be sent back on the next boat to China! And the methods they used were tricky. Questions were asked nonstop, one after another under a glaring light, and the key questions were repeated over and over again to catch any inconsistencies. And of course they expected quick answers—who would not know his own parents' names at the snap of a finger? Luckily, my paper was fairly simple; it was for a single person with no family or obligations. This meant that there was less to memorize and less possibility of a slipup. I could have purchased a paper for a married man with two sons, but that would have meant more names and dates to memorize. Opting for a single-person paper meant that I could not bring my sons over to the United States, but that was not my objective. Like all other Gold Mountain [an immigrant term for America] dreamers, I wanted to make my fortune and return home a wealthy and envied man.

My real father, already in Gold Mountain as a paper son himself, made my passage to America possible. He informed me of the availability of this particular paper and then, in a manner befitting a spy novel, I obtained it from the "agent" in my village. My father also managed to borrow enough money from a distant cousin to finance my trip. My paper, at a cost of $100 for each year recorded— that is, each year of my age—cost me $2,000 with fee, excluding transportation. This I was able to purchase on credit and would repay when I arrived and found work.

Late in the summer of 1934, after three days of intensive interrogation in a dingy little room at the Boston Immigration House, I walked away a United States citizen. I was now a Gold Mountain man and had broken the bonds of poverty that marked the Sha-tou villagers! Yet I knew that I had a long way to go before I could call myself a free man, for I was overburdened with debt. I was excited, though, eager, and most of all determined. I learned to iron shirts and within two months was hired out in Providence, Rhode Island, at $8 a week.

First Jobs

Mr. Chin was my first employer.

"How long have you been here, Uncle Chin?"

"Forty years," he said.

"And you have never gone back to see the old woman?"

"What is the use of seeing the old woman?" he retorted.

"I have a son there, he got married and got me grandsons. I bought acres of rice fields, built a new house, and now I send money home to bring up all the grandchildren." He enumerated them proudly. As I sat listening to him, I felt sad for him—and for myself and my future. I wondered if this would be my fate, too. For like everyone else in my village, I had visions of someday returning home in grandeur. . . .

Uncle Chin was very stingy. During the two weeks that I worked for him, what we ate were pork bellies cooked with shrimp sauce and two bowls of rice. He kept a glass jar of bean curds underneath the stack of starch crates that were covered up with an old unclaimed sheet to serve as a dining table. During the morning and night meals he would eat his bowl of rice. Then he took out the jar from underneath the crates, opened it, and with his pair of soiled chopsticks, picked out a piece of bean curd and deposited it into his rice bowl. The cost of one piece of bean curd was less than a penny, but he never offered me one. I never got enough to eat when I worked for Uncle Chin.

After completing my second week with him I returned to Boston and got a new job with Uncle Lee in Somerville at $15 a week. The fall weather was setting in, and I, being from the southernmost tip of China, was not prepared for the weather changes of the northeastern United States.

"You have no overcoat in this kind of weather?" Lee asked me.

"No. I have no money to afford one," I said.

"I lend you mine," he said plainly. When I put on the coat its length reached my ankles and the sleeves covered my fingertips. I wore his coat every Sunday for the entire fall and winter. . . .

Taking Over Father's Laundry

I worked for Uncle Lee for nearly half a year, through the summer of 1935. I ate good food at his laundry and got $15 in weekly wages. I was also learning a lot more about life in Gold Mountain.

One Sunday my father called me and asked me to take over his laundry. At age fifty-seven, he was ill. . . .

My father's laundry was located at 87 Chelsea Street in Charlestown, Massachusetts. The store was very small, about ten feet by fifteen feet. One-third of the space was used as a drying room, and in this space stood a sink, a portable gas range, and a coal stove for drying shirts. On the ceiling were some wires attached at each end to two wooden two-by-fours nailed to the wall; the wires were used for hanging shirts. In the extreme left corner was a stairway that led to the basement, where a ton of coal was stored in the corner to the right; the toilet was to the left. He slept at night on a board, two feet by six feet, suspended by heavy wire from the ceiling—a sort of wooden hammock! I slept in the drying room on a wooden board positioned on top of two wooden horses that we used as stepladders when hanging shirts from the ceiling. The wallpaper was blackened and peeling from the moisture in the air. The chief reason why laundry men could afford to go back to the homeland once every few years was that they were able to save money on rent and transportation by living in their laundries.

Now, business for this particular laundry, which was near a navy yard, had been good. But an old friend of my father's with a big family opened a laundry two blocks away at the top of Bunker Hill, and my father's business soon fell off—in fact, it dwindled to almost nothing. When people asked this old friend why he had to open a laundry so close to his good friend and "break his rice bowl," he replied, "This is Gold Mountain. I have the freedom to do business wherever I choose!" His friend was right. He had learned the secrets of free enterprise.

Paper Son

"The paper I arranged for your passage to the United States cost $2,000; the boat and train expenses were about another $400. That is a total of $2,400. Have you paid back any money to Yu Nap?" my father inquired the first night we met at his laundry. "After all, you have come to the United States nearly a year ago now."

Yu Nap is the second son of my father's third brother. He came to this country in his early twenties, first as a paper son, but gave the wrong answer at Immigration and broke the contract. He returned one year later as the son of a merchant, which meant that he had the right to come in once but not to reenter if for any reason he left the country. He tried to marry in the United States, but his mother picked a girl for him in China and told him that if he did not come home, she would hang herself. He finally did return, but his father-in-law managed to find him another paper son contract, for one old enough not to be inducted into the army in the event of another world war.

"I have not and cannot pay him anything yet. You know that I make only $15 a week [which was top pay for hired help in the laundry business in 1935], and when I come out to Chinatown on Sundays you always demand half of it as gambling money. As for the rest of the money, I have a family back home to support. I don't even have money to buy a winter coat. This ragged coat was given to me, worn out to the sleeves, by Cousin Sing Tu when he asked and discovered I had none. Before this, I only borrowed Uncle Lee's.

"You know, as a hired help to Uncle Lee I ate good food and earned $15 a week. Why do you call me back here when you have only twenty some odd dollars of business yourself? You have come to the United States more than ten years now, and you have not contributed a penny toward this paper. To pay back all this debt I have to work fifteen or more years," I said.

"Oh, don't worry. You don't have to pay Yu Nap the whole amount before going home for a visit. I want you to know that I did my best to get you here. In the first place Yu Nap wanted to get his brother here. When he came and asked me for my opinion, I told him that I am too old and could not help him in any way. So he changed his mind and got a paper suitable for your age. It costs $100 for each year of your age. It wasn't stated in the paper either that you were married and have two sons because it would cost even more. Besides, there would be more questions to answer in the paper. As for this laundry, I know it is a financial loss to you, but I paid $1,500 for it. It is my hope that business will pick up again some day. You've got to learn that to be a one-penny boss is better than to be a two-penny hire-out," he said. He was right in this sense, and so for the time being I remained at my father's laundry, my own boss.

Life in Chinatown

Bruce Edward Hall

Many American cities developed large ethnic enclaves called "Chinatowns," where Chinese immigrant families put down roots. In this passage from his family memoir, *Tea That Burns*, fourth-generation Chinese American Bruce Edward Hall tells the story of his own extended family's life on Mott Street in New York City's Chinatown in the 1920s. Hall, whose family name Hor was changed to Hall in 1950, describes the close-knit Chinese community in New York during that era when everyone knew each other and everyone watched out for each other's children. Hall is a freelance writer and the author of *Diamond Street: The Story of the Little Town with the Big Red Light District*.

The old men with the queues and the loose-fitting blouses are rapidly disappearing, being replaced by a new generation that is dragging Chinatown into the 20th century. The Chinese population citywide stands at about five thousand in 1920, up from ten years previously but still well below the 1900 level. But at least there has been peace in the neighborhood for the last few years, as the various warring factions have found it seemly to pause for World War I. In keeping with Chinatown's newfound spirit of patriotism, Lee B. Lok, in conjunction with the Chinatown Chamber of Commerce, had been selling war bonds right over the herb counter of Quong Yuen Shing [a Chinese general store] eventually raising over a million dollars. Of course, the Chinese are known for their support of civic causes. . . .

Still, for all the peace and stability, some white people are beginning to find Chinatown rather dull. To be sure, the big, gasping tour buses are back in force, doing the circuit of curio shop to Chinese temple to chopsuey house, with a running narration of Tong Wars [conflict among Chinese criminal gangs] and degradation shouted through a megaphone. But opium was finally declared illegal, at least for recreational use, in 1914, and this year the hated Volstead Act has come into effect, ushering in more than ten years of Prohibition in the nation and essentially shutting down the Bowery dives so popular with slummers for decades past. Of course, opium and liquor are still obtainable—the Tongs have even started selling string soaked in heroin, sold by the inch and meant to be chewed—but that is mostly for the residents' use, and Chinatown and its environs no longer have that allure of shimmering vice beckoning to adventurers from uptown and other foreign climes. That is just fine with the residents of the old neighborhood, who are getting sick and tired of being stereotyped as opium fiends and Tong hatchet men. When a movie crew is found to be shooting a typically sinister white-slavery potboiler on Doyers Street in 1923, the locals respond by pelting the actors with eggs and rotten vegetables. . . .

Head of the Family

As for my family, the death of Hor Poa [author's great-grandfather] leaves them somewhat in limbo. Great-Grandfather has left the bulk of his estate to his sons in China. Unfortunately, the elder son, Hor Mei Wong, doesn't survive his father very long, apparently succumbing to tuberculosis right there on Mott Street before he can ever get back home. But Hor Mei Fun inherits the big house in the middle of the family compound and all the money, making him, according to village elders, "very wealthy." Re-

portedly, he even starts his own bank when he moves back
to China for good in the later 1920s, although by American
standards that doesn't necessarily make him a tycoon. At
any rate, Hor Mei Wong's wife and children get the house on
one side of the family compound, and Hor Mei Chao, the
son of Hor Poa's long-dead younger brother, gets the house
on the other side. Thus, the family Hor is snug and secure
in their little ancestral village, enjoying the life of provincial
gentry, and for the moment, pass out of the story.

But the pressure on Grandfather [Hor Ting Pun, called
"Hock Shop"] only increases. Every two years there has
been a baby, and by 1923, our household at 33–37 Mott con-
sists of Great-Grandmother Gon She, 43; Grandfather, 26;
Grandmother Chin She, 27; Third Great-Uncle Hor Ting
Sun, 17; Fourth Great-Uncle Hor Ting Fong, 14; Great-Aunt
Hor Yee Bik, 10; First Aunt Thelma Bo Choi, 8, Second
Aunt Constance Bo Ling, 6; First Uncle Everett Sing Ying,
4; Third Aunt Frances Bo Ping, 2; plus my Father, Herbert
Sing Nuen, born that year on the second day of June.
Twelve people. Three rooms. One income from Grandfa-
ther's job as a waiter; and, to complicate matters, Second
Aunt Constance has been left totally deaf from a bout of
scarlet fever at the age of two, which means that soon she
will need to go to a special school. To help out, Great-Uncle
Sun drops out of Stuyvesant High in his senior year and gets
a job as a waiter, but his older brother, my grandfather, is
only furious with him for quitting school.

Hor Ting Pun makes anywhere from $100 to $150 per
month in his waiter's job, probably at the lavish Oriental
Restaurant on Pell Street, which is owned by Hor family
"cousins." While respectable for the early 1920s, his salary
has to stretch awfully far, and besides he feels that he is too
intelligent to be trapped in some grunt job. A restaurant
worker's day grinds on from opening to closing, about fourteen hours a day, although there is time for a break during

slow periods. Small restaurants, like the little basement noodle shops favored by most Chinese, might be run by three partners—two cooks and a manager/waiter. The percentage of their share of the profits is according to the size of their initial investment. If business is good, a part-time waiter, maybe a college student, can be hired at $2 or $3 a day on weekends, which is always the busiest time. With tips, a part-timer can earn up to $10 a day. . . .

Chinese Social Life

The three-room apartment wasn't quite as claustrophobic as it sounds, because, like every building in Chinatown, 33–37 Mott was merely a vertical Chinese village. All the doors were always open, and everyone moved freely from apartment to apartment. The women could have a social life without leaving the building, while the children actually had dozens of mothers and fathers, as they were raised to strictly defer to any elder person, whom they would invariably address as "Auntie" or "Uncle." And there certainly was no shortage of elders in their little world.

There was the lady downstairs on the third floor who had bound feet. One of my father's earliest memories is a grotesque vision of those feet, unbound, propped up on a chair—two fists of flesh, with seemingly one toe each. Her husband owned a grocery store on Mott Street and a farm in Boonton, New Jersey, where he grew Chinese vegetables. Sometimes he would take the children out there in his car, where they would sleep on mats on the floor and roam the unfamiliar surroundings. It often seemed as though half of Chinatown was taking the air at his farm.

Then there was Mr. Chin, who made beautiful kites in the shapes of fish, dragons, or caterpillars which could stretch up to twelve feet in length. The paste he would make himself, boiling rice into a sticky mush and then pounding it fine. The struts came from bamboo packing cases carrying goods imported from China. The eyes, scales, and whiskers would be delicately painted by hand. Mr. Chin would take the children down to Columbus Park, or more often up to the roof, where his creations could sail over Mott Street like some brilliantly-colored good-luck omen beaming on the lives below. When they strayed over Mulberry Street, however, the Italian kids would try to bring the kites down with rocks and lassos, savagely ripping apart any that they caught. Mr. Chin would just sigh and go down to make another one.

Miss Mary Banta was such a frequent visitor to 33–37 that she might as well have lived there. She would come by and try to teach English to Chin She and Gon She, who apparently never made any headway. The children she would check for lice or illness, sweeping them off to the doctor at the slightest sign of a sniffle. Sometimes her Church of

Chinese immigrants often settled in established ethnic communities known as Chinatowns, such as this one on Mott Street in New York City.

All Nations would sponsor steamboat excursions up to Bear Mountain—just for Chinese—and the family, or at least the children, would clamber aboard with a big bucket of chicken gizzards and deep-fried chicken feet as tasty snacks. And for two weeks every summer, the church would host the Chinese at a seaside resort they owned in Bradley Beach, New Jersey.

There were also other kids living at 33–37, like "Little Pig" and "Pee Wee"—all Chinese children had these affectionate "milk names," although my elders would resolutely never tell me theirs—and they would amuse themselves on the streets, on the roofs, in the alleys. Just as for the adults, one of a Chinese child's chief forms of recreation was eating, and when out of sight of their parents there was much to choose from, like the roasted sweet potatoes from the Italian street vendor who worked Mott Street, at a penny apiece, or two cents for the big ones, with an aroma so delicious you could smell them coming a block away. Or there were the men selling roasted corn on the cob, or knishes, or steamed snails, or lemon tea. Then, when fortified by such nourishment, the kids would run over to Columbus Park to play volleyball or softball, often ending up in a turf battle with some Italian boys, who would snarl at them to "go back to your own neighborhood." Only when the boundaries were finally established could the game proceed.

Family Outings

There were occasions when the entire family would venture outside together, although it had to be something very important for Gon She and Chin She, being conservative ladies, to brave the harsh glare of a public street. Uncle Everett can still recall a visit to a First Son's party in 1924 when he was only five, but then, as a First Son himself, he would be an honored guest. As for his mother and grandmother, he remembers them stepping gingerly onto the sidewalk, dressed to the nines in clothes he had never seen before, gorgeous silks and dainty shoes, with their hair done up in elaborate coifs held in place by big hair pins like knitting needles. Once they were safely out onto the street a taxi pulled up, the party climbed in, the taxi drove to a building on the opposite curb, and the party climbed out. Even at this late date strict propriety must be maintained, and well into the 1930s boys would sit on the stoop and play a game called "count the women." There were so few, and they came out so infrequently, that the boys soon knew all of them by sight.

Other more liberal families would take a Sunday meal out together, usually not at one of the big eating palaces but at some more humble noodle house serving good Cantonese food. In the middle 1920s, the Nom Wah (Southern China) Tea Parlor opened at 13–15 Doyers, filling up the whole end of what had once been the Arcade that went through to Mott. The police had ordered the Arcade, as well as all the tunnels running underneath, sealed off in an attempt to curb Tong shenanigans.

Nom Wah serves only *yum cha*, or tea food, which is what they called dim sum back then. I know that Grandfather used to hang out there with his friends, and Nom Wah, still in business in the late 1990s, is another place where I have always seen familiar ghosts. There are still the old, worn red booths, and the row of tall gas-fired hot-water urns supported on their little curvy legs. On one wall are framed views of British-colonial Shanghai, which might be photographs, might be needlework, the covering glass being just a little too dusty to tell. There are shelves of beautiful painted-tin tea canisters, reaching all the way to the ceiling. Colorful chinaware household gods beam down from behind glass cases piled high with homemade almond cookies. And a single waiter still carries around big trays of tea food for you to select from, such as steamed roast-pork dumplings known as *char siu bao; siu mai*, or little balls of steamed ground pork and fish; the square fried turnip cakes called *lo bok gao;* little shrimp *ha gao;* and all sorts of other things that I've never quite figured out. There is no bill, so when the meal is over the owner just comes over and counts up the empty dishes, each size and shape denoting a different price.

Chinatown Entertainment

There are other sources of entertainment for Hock Shop and his friends in the 1920s, such as the new Chinese Theater, on the Bowery above Bayard Street in the old Thalia, which had once been famous as the first theater in New York to be lit by gas. The bill is largely the same as in the old place on Doyers, with long classical fables and history plays. The seats are also the same—wooden benches, "backless and uncomfortable." The prices have gone up, however—from $2 for early arrivals to a low of 50 cents if you get there after ten. Still it might be worth it to go and see the first Chinese-American actress, a woman by the name of Ng Ah.

There is also dancing at the Oriental Restaurant. Obviously, Grandfather himself wouldn't socialize there if that's where he was waiting on tables, but some young Chinese can occasionally be seen among the uptown crowd dancing to the "syncopating jazz orchestra," even though there is a warning sign over the piano reading, "No Charleston." Bootleg Tea That Burns [illegal liquor] flows like water, as the young men of Chinatown learn to roar with the Twenties.

Seeking Independence

Jade Snow Wong

Jade Snow Wong was born in 1922 into a Chinese immigrant family living in California. Despite the fact that her father wanted his children to become educated, he made it clear that he would give financial support only to his first-born son. In consequence, Wong determined to work her way through college. In school in 1938 she was exposed to the idea that modern Americans have rights and do not always have to obey parents unquestioningly. In this passage from Wong's memoir, *Fifth Chinese Daughter*, she describes a confrontation she had with her parents regarding her desire to go out with a male classmate. Her parents were angry because she did not first ask their permission. Wong writes her story in the third person because, as she explains in the introduction to the book, she is following the traditional "Chinese literary form (reflecting cultural disregard for the individual)." Wong went on to graduate Phi Beta Kappa from Mills College in Oakland, California, with honors in sociology and economics. The second volume of her autobiography, *No Chinese Stranger*, was published in 1975.

Jade Snow was delighted. Her first movie with Joe! What a wonderful day. In happy anticipation she put on her long silk stockings, lipstick, and the nearest thing to a suit she owned—a hand-me-down jacket and a brown skirt she had made herself. Then with a bright ribbon tying back her long black hair she was ready.

Daddy didn't miss a detail of the preparations as she dashed from room to room. He waited until she was finished before he demanded, "Jade Snow, where are you going?"

"I am going out into the street," she answered.

"Did you ask my permission to go out into the street?"

"No, Daddy."

"Do you have your mother's permission to go out into the street?"

"No, Daddy."

A sudden silence from the kitchen indicated that Mama was listening.

Daddy went on: "Where and when did you learn to be so daring as to leave this house without permission of your parents? You did not learn it under my roof."

It was all very familiar. Jade Snow waited, knowing that Daddy had not finished. In a moment he came to the point.

"And with whom are you going out into the street?"

It took all the courage Jade Snow could muster, remembering her new thinking, to say nothing. It was certain that if she told Daddy that she was going out with a boy whom he did not know, without a chaperone, he would be convinced that she would lose her maidenly purity before the evening was over.

"Very well," Daddy said sharply. "If you will not tell me, I forbid you to go! You are now too old to whip."

That was the moment.

Children as Individuals

Suppressing all anger, and in a manner that would have done credit to her sociology instructor addressing his freshman class, Jade Snow carefully turned on her mentally rehearsed speech.

"That is something you should think more about. Yes, I am too old to whip. I am too old to be treated as a child. I can now think for myself, and you and Mama should not demand unquestioning obedience from me. You should understand me. There was a time in America when parents raised children to make them work, but now the foreigners regard them as individuals with rights of their own. I have worked too, but now I am an individual besides being your fifth daughter."

It was almost certain that Daddy blinked, but after the briefest pause he gathered himself together.

"Where," he demanded, "did you learn such an unfilial theory?"

Mama had come quietly into the room and slipped into a chair to listen.

"From my teacher," Jade Snow answered triumphantly, "who you taught me is supreme after you, and whose judgment I am not to question."

Daddy was feeling pushed. Thoroughly aroused, he shouted:

"A little learning has gone to your head! How can you permit a foreigner's theory to put aside the practical experience of the Chinese, who for thousands of years have preserved a most superior family pattern? Confucius had already presented an organized philosophy of manners and conduct when the foreigners were unappreciatively persecuting Christ. Who brought you up? Who clothed you, fed you, sheltered you, nursed you? Do you think you were born aged sixteen? You owe honor to us before you satisfy your personal whims."

Daddy thundered on, while Jade Snow kept silent.

"What would happen to the order of this household if each of you four children started to behave like individuals? Would we have one peaceful moment if your personal desires came before your duty? How could we maintain our self-respect if we, your parents, did not know where you were at night and with whom you were keeping company?"

With difficulty Jade Snow kept herself from being swayed by fear and the old familiar arguments. "You can be bad in the daytime as well as at night," she said defensively. "What could happen after eleven that couldn't happen before?"

The Family's Reputation

Daddy was growing more excited. "Do I have to justify my judgment to you? I do not want a daughter of mine to be known as one who walks the streets at night. Have you no thought for our reputations if not for your own? If you start going out with boys, no good man will want to ask you to be his wife. You just do not know as well as we do what is good for you."

Mama fanned Daddy's wrath, "Never having been a mother, you cannot know how much grief it is to bring up a daughter. Of course we will not permit you to run the risk of corrupting your purity before marriage."

"Oh, Mama!" Jade Snow retorted. "This is America, not China. Don't you think I have any judgment? How can you think I would go out with just any man?"

"Men!" Daddy roared. "You don't know a thing about them. I tell you, you can't trust any of them."

Now it was Jade Snow who felt pushed. She delivered the balance of her declaration of independence:

"Both of you should understand that I am growing up to be a woman in a society greatly different from the one you knew in China. You expect me to work my way through college—which would not have been possible in China. You expect me to exercise judgment in choosing my employers and my jobs and in spending my own money in the American world. Then why can't I choose my friends? Of course independence is not safe. But safety isn't the only consideration. You must give me the freedom to find some answers for myself."

Mama found her tongue first. "You think you are too good for us because you have a little foreign book knowledge."

"You will learn the error of your ways after it is too late," Daddy added darkly.

A Daughter's Victory

By this Jade Snow knew that her parents had conceded defeat. Hoping to soften the blow, she tried to explain: "If I am to earn my living, I must learn how to get along with many kinds of people, with foreigners as well as Chinese. I intend to start finding out about them now. You must have confidence that I shall remain true to the spirit of your teachings. I shall bring back to you the new knowledge of whatever I learn."

Daddy and Mama did not accept this offer graciously. "It is as useless for you to tell me such ideas as 'The wind blows across a deaf ear.' You have lost your sense of balance," Daddy told her bluntly, "You are shameless. Your skin is yellow. Your features are forever Chinese. We are content with our proven ways. Do not try to force foreign ideas into my home. Go. You will one day tell us sorrowfully that you have been mistaken."

After that there was no further discussion of the matter. Jade Snow came and went without any questions being asked. In spite of her parents' dark predictions, her new freedom in the choice of companions did not result in a rush of undesirables. As a matter of fact, the boys she met at school were more concerned with copying her lecture notes than with anything else.

CHAPTER 3

World War II and Beyond

COMING TO AMERICA

World War II and Chinese American Women

Xiaojian Zhao

In this selection from her book *Remaking Chinese America*, Xiaojian Zhao describes the changes that World War II brought to the Chinese American community, especially to Chinese American women. The United States entered World War II in 1941 when the Japanese attacked Pearl Harbor. China, which had been invaded by Japan in 1937, immediately became an ally of the United States, and the two countries joined to fight Japanese aggression. Out of respect for this alliance, American anti-Chinese laws came under review by U.S. legislators. For example, the 1882 Chinese Exclusion Act, which severely restricted Chinese immigration, was overturned in 1943. Chinese Americans were encouraged to join the U.S. war effort by serving in the military and by working in the defense industry.

These wartime changes had dramatic effects on Chinese American women. Prior to the war, most Chinese American women adhered to traditional roles by staying at home and caring for their families. If they worked, their jobs were in the family business. After the war broke out, however, Chinese American women began working in defense factories, holding jobs that American men had held before entering the military. These jobs put Chinese American women in contact with Americans of all ethnic backgrounds and opened doors that had previously been closed. Moreover, Chinese American women gained greater personal control over their money and their time. Zhao is

Xiaojian Zhao, *Remaking Chinese America: Immigration, Family, and Community, 1940–1965*. New Brunswick, NJ: Rutgers University Press, 2002. Copyright © 2002 by Rutgers University Press. Reproduced by permission.

associate professor at the University of California, Santa Barbara, and the author of several books and articles on Chinese American history.

World War II profoundly changed the lives of Chinese American women. For the first time, the larger American society welcomed the contributions of most ethnic and gender minorities. Chinese American women entered the armed forces and were hired by industries previously dominated by white males; they worked side by side with men and women of different ethnic backgrounds. The war altered American attitudes toward Chinese in the United States as well as the Chinese community's attitudes toward women. The Chinese American women who participated in the war effort found themselves even more changed. The story of their involvement in the war is not just the story of how much they contributed to the war effort. It is also the story of the creation of a new generation of Chinese American women.

The Prewar Experience

There were more male Chinese than female Chinese in the United States before World War II: 285 males for every 100 females in 1940. Because laborers' wives were barred during the Chinese exclusion,[1] a fairly large number of female Chinese immigrants were wives of men who had merchant status. Few of these women's families were affluent, however. Many merchants' wives started to work immediately after they arrived, and most Chinese business owners would not have been able to make ends meet without the free labor provided by their spouses.

While wives of Chinese merchants labored alongside

---

1. Almost all Chinese were denied entry into the United States under the Chinese Exclusion Act of 1882.

their husbands in family-operated businesses whenever they were not occupied with household duties, most wives of Chinese laborers found work sewing, canning fruit, or shelling shrimp. The flexible working arrangements of Chinese-operated businesses made it possible for women to combine wage earning with family obligations. In Chinatown garment shops, babies slept in little cribs next to their mothers' sewing machines, and toddlers crawled around on the floor. Many women also did piecework at home. These arrangements were important in maintaining the traditional order of the family and community. Women were paid lower hourly wages than men, and they had to shoulder many household responsibilities. Not until the early 1940s did nursery schools begin to appear in San Francisco's Chinatown. Few Chinese American families, however, were accustomed to the idea of leaving their children at childcare facilities. Nor did most Chinese women in the United States have their parents nearby to help out with childcare, which left them as their children's primary caretaker. While Chinese men were free to play a large role in the community, the double burden of wage earning and household responsibility kept women occupied.

The isolation of the Chinese community also limited Chinese women's dealings with the outside world. In the late 1930s, only 4 percent of the Chinese families in San Francisco had cars, and few women knew how to drive. Most immigrant women living in Chinatowns in large cities were familiar only with the areas within walking distance of their homes. Some never ventured outside their communities without their husbands.

The 1900 U.S. Census recorded 2,353 Chinese females living in the country who either were born in the United States or had gained derivative citizenship from their fathers, but these women, too, found their lives isolated. Ah Yoke Gee's father, Jung San Choy, was a pioneering fisherman in the Monterey Bay area. Ah Yoke grew up in the small Chinese fishing community there, lived in San Francisco's Chinatown after she got married, and later settled down in a racially mixed neighborhood in Berkeley with her family. Even though she could read and drive, Ah Yoke found her life was confined within the Chinese American community. She was a member of Berkeley's Chinese Presbyterian Church and a frequenter of San Francisco's Chinatown. In 1930, after her husband died, Ah Yoke became the breadwinner for a family of six children. She took in sewing through a Chinese subcontractor in Oakland and worked at home while taking care of her offspring.

Most American-born Chinese women of Ah Yoke's age had little education, and many of them did not receive any public schooling whatsoever because they were systematically rejected by the public school system. Some went to segregated schools, the first of which was established in 1859 in San Francisco. After the facility was closed down by the school board in 1871, however, the city's Chinese children were excluded from public education for fourteen years. In 1885 the California Supreme Court ruled in *Tape v. Hurley* that Chinese children were entitled to public education, but the San Francisco Board of Education successfully campaigned to pass a state law imposing separate education on these students. The segregation of black children, in contrast, had ended ten years earlier. Following San Francisco's example, several other districts in the Bay Area also established segregated schools for Chinese pupils.

Educational Opportunities for Women

By the 1920s, however, school segregation policies were breaking down and younger Chinese American children were gaining access to public education. Most Chinese American women who came of age on the eve of World War II had gone to high school, and some had attended college. As Ah Yoke Gee's daughter, Maggie Gee, recalled, going to college seemed to be a way of life for youngsters in Berkeley, where the central campus of the University of California was located. Her family was by no means affluent, but to save money Maggie lived at home while enrolled in the university, and she paid the twenty-eight-dollar quarterly fees and bought school supplies out of her own earnings from odd jobs. Ah Yoke never dreamed of higher education for herself, but sending Maggie to college was simply a matter of "setting her daughter's bowl of rice on the table" a few years longer, and she could not say no. Jade Snow Wong, who received no financial assistance from her parents, went through college on a scholarship and the wages from a part-time job. Aimei Chen, the daughter of a Chinese restaurant waiter, enrolled in a community college in Stockton, California. She did not know what she would do with a college degree, but since she did not have a full-time job, she decided to take advantage of the opportunity.

The educational opportunities available at the time differentiated this generation of Chinese American women from their mothers. The racially diverse educational institutions provided them not only with academic knowledge but also with experiences that encouraged their desire for more equitable race and gender relations. In the classroom, Chinese women competed with their non-Chinese peers, and some excelled academically. They learned that they had rights as individuals and deserved respect from others. . . .

By 1940 the number of American-born Chinese women was almost triple that of their parents' generation. Within the community, however, they could find employment only in places such as garment shops, laundries, canneries, and restaurants, the same businesses where their mothers had worked.

Many Chinese children grew up working alongside their mothers. Jade Snow Wong began working in her family's garment shop when she was ten, helping load clothes on pick-up days. By age eleven, she had a sewing machine next to her mother's. Elizabeth Lew, Lew Chuck Suey's granddaughter, remembered her mother's job as a routine activity in which all family members except for her father participated. Her mother usually sewed dresses while the children worked on jeans. Those who were not tall enough to operate the sewing machine helped snip the threads. Elizabeth learned to sew at almost the same time she learned to read, and it was not long before she was hired in a garment shop in Oakland's Chinatown. . . .

Employment Opportunities for Women

Aimei Chen, who had come to the United States in her infancy as a paper daughter,[2] grew up in the small Chinese community in Stockton. She worked as a waitress in a Chinese café while attending junior college. Other girls her age were hired by local dime-stores, ice-cream parlors, and department stores, but none of the jobs were available to a Chinese girl. Taking business classes in college, she did not think much of her future. It was unlikely that she would find a job outside her community, and Stockton's Chinatown was too small to provide full-time employment for Chinese women.

Yulan Liu, who was born in Oakland, was a grocery clerk's daughter. She began working in a laundry when she was twelve, following in her mother's footsteps. She never had time to play with other children, and she did not recall ever having been invited to a house outside the Chinese community.

The educated young Chinese women had higher expectations than their mothers, however. They would not be

2. Many Chinese immigrants entered the United States between 1882 and 1943 (the era of the Chinese Exclusion Act of 1882) by using forged documents. These immigrants were known as "paper sons" and "paper daughters."

satisfied by working at the same jobs as their mothers, marrying young, and having numerous children. Some girls planned to go to China for their future careers; others hoped that one day the world outside academic institutions would also recognize and reward individual merit.

World War II: The Turning Point

Ironically it was the attack on Pearl Harbor, one of the most tragic events in the history of the United States, that allowed Chinese Americans to take part in the larger society. On December 7, 1941, Maggie Gee went to study in the campus library. As she entered the usually quiet reading room, she was surprised to see that no one was reading. People were talking loudly and emotionally. Maggie sensed that something important had happened, and she soon learned of the Japanese bombing of Pearl Harbor in Hawaii.

For Chinese Americans, World War II had begun when the Japanese invaded Manchuria, in northeastern China, on September 18, 1931. Maggie was a fourth grader at the time. She and her sister had planned a trip to China with their uncle, but the trip was canceled after the Japanese invasion. When the Japanese attacked Chinese troops at Lugou qiao (Marco Polo Bridge) near Beijing on July 7, 1937, the war against Japan was joined by overseas Chinese in most parts of the world. Maggie and her siblings accompanied their mother to many rallies and fund-raising drives in San Francisco's Chinatown. She was extremely upset by the atrocities that took place during the 1937 Nanjing Massacre.[3] She was surprised and disturbed that her classmates knew little about what was going on in China and also by their lack of interest in what had happened. Pearl Harbor, however, brought China and the United States together against a common enemy. Suddenly everyone was talking

3. For six weeks in 1937, Japanese troops occupied Nanjing and committed horrible atrocities against the civilian population. As many as 350,000 citizens were murdered.

about the war. Maggie's support of the war effort in China became an indication of her loyalty to the United States.

Many Chinese Americans have mixed feelings about World War II. Without the bombing of Pearl Harbor, the isolation of the Chinese American community would have lasted much longer. During the war Japanese Americans were seen as enemy aliens and were sent to internment camps. Because resistance against the Japanese was crucial to the Allied victory, the Chinese people were portrayed positively by the American media. On December 22, 1941, a short article was published in *Time* magazine to help Americans differentiate their Chinese "friends" from the Japanese. According to the magazine, the facial expressions of the Chinese were more "placid, kindly, open"; those of the Japanese were more "positive, dogmatic, arrogant." World War II, considered by the American public to be a "good war" against fascists who had launched a racist war, put pressure on the government to improve its domestic race relations. Discriminatory legislation against the Chinese in the United States . . . was an embarrassment to the United States during its wartime alliance with China. Chinese Americans, too, recognized the racial dimension of this war. "It is fortunate," said an editorial in the *Chinese Times*, "that this war has the white race and the yellow race on both sides and therefore will not turn into a war between the two."

The wartime shortage of workers helped lower racial barriers in the military service and in the defense industry. In May 1942, defense establishments in the San Francisco Bay Area began advertising jobs in local Chinese newspapers. The Kaiser shipyards in Richmond announced that they would hire Chinese regardless of their citizenship status or English skills. In a recruiting speech, corporation president Henry J. Kaiser urged Chinese to work in his shipyards to support the war effort. The Moore

Dry Dock Company in Oakland hired Chinese-speaking instructors in its welding school and provided a shuttle bus service between the shipyard and Oakland's Chinatown for Chinese trainees.

After decades of isolation imposed by anti-Chinese legislation and sentiment, the Chinese American community lost no time in seizing these opportunities. Participation in the war effort could build up the nation's defense and help defeat the enemies of both China and the United States. Military service would qualify Chinese immigrants for U.S. citizenship, breaking through the restrictions of the exclusion acts. Employment in defense industries, suggested the *Chinese Times*, also paid well and could be used for draft deferment. Moreover, defense-employees could apply for government-subsidized housing, which would afford Chinese Americans the rare opportunity to move out of Chinatowns. Thousands of Chinese American men and women answered the government's call. Their wartime employment would forever change their own lives as well as the development of the community.

Work in Defense Plants

News reports and oral history interviews suggest that by 1943, about five thousand Chinese Americans were at work in defense jobs in the San Francisco Bay Area, and between five and six hundred of them were women. Chinese American women in other parts of California and around the nation also joined in defense work, especially in Los Angeles, Portland, Seattle, Chicago, New York, and Boston.

Chinese American women were a familiar sight at most defense plants in the Bay Area. As early as May 1942, the *Chinese Press* reported that eighteen-year-old Ruth Law was the youngest office staff member at Engineer Supply Depot, Pier 90, and her co-worker Anita Lee was an assistant to the company's chief clerk. Fannie Yee, a high school senior, won the top secretary award at the Bethlehem Steel Corporation local headquarters in San Francisco. In Oakland, Stella Quan was recognized by Army Supply. Both Jenny Sui of San Francisco and Betty Choy of Vallejo started as messenger girls in the Mare Island shipyard, but they were quickly promoted to clerk-typists. Before Kaiser's shipyards in Richmond and Bechtel's Marinship in Sausalito began production work, the Moore Dry Dock Company in Oakland, the Naval Air Base in Alameda, the Mare Island Navy Shipyard, and the Army Department at Fort Mason in San Francisco were the primary defense employers for Chinese women.

The majority of the Chinese American women who joined in defense work had grown up in the United States. Of the seventy-six named in published sources and the twenty-four interviewed, only four were over the age of forty at the time of the war and very few were married. With relatively few household responsibilities, these women had the freedom and independence to work outside the home.

It was the combination of economic opportunity and patriotism that led Chinese women to work in defense jobs. When Ah Yoke Gee was forty-six, employment outside the Chinese American community became possible for the first time, and she jumped at the chance to serve the country of her birth. Elizabeth Low was hired at the Naval Air Base in Alameda, making twenty-five dollars a week, four times more than she had made in the sewing factory. Defense employment was an undreamed-of opportunity for Aimei Chen. With her college education, she landed a secretarial job at the Stockton Army Depot. Yulan Liu had just graduated from high school in the summer of 1942 when her brother got a job at Moore Dry Dock Company and encouraged her to try as well. Yulan went to the yard the next day and became a welder.

Married women had to find ways to combine work and household responsibilities. Because her youngest child was already in high school, Ah Yoke Gee's household chores were manageable. Working the swing shift in the shipyard, she cooked the whole day's food in the morning, and shopped and did the laundry on Sundays. Jane Jeong, married for only four months, took a job at Richmond Shipyard Number Two. Her husband was a merchant seaman, so Jane was free to work outside the home. . . .

The Benefits of Wartime Employment

Wartime employment brought tangible benefits to many Chinese Americans. Although Chinese American women had labored hard at home and outside the home before the war, their productivity was neither recognized nor rewarded. Many girls had no say in discussions about spending the money they gave to their families. Elizabeth Lew had worked with her sister in a garment factory since she was ten to supplement her family income. "Payday Pearl and I would go to the Safeway store on the way home," she recalled. "Payday we would spend three cents each" for a push-up popsicle. During the war several of Elizabeth's sisters and brothers were employed by defense plants, which helped pull their family out of poverty. Elizabeth finally had a little money to call her own. She spent many Sundays in movie theaters and at an ice rink. "For people who used to have very little money," said Aimei Chen, "the war was a time of great economic opportunity." She brought home kitchenware and other household items, things that were considered luxuries in the past, and she was free to purchase clothing she liked.

Compared with their jobs before the war, most Chinese women found the so-called men's jobs easy. Joy Yee, a San Francisco-born high school graduate, was the second daughter of an Oakland garment shop owner. She and her sisters had sewed in the shop, but her mother told Joy that she was no good at sewing and that she would never succeed as a seamstress. At Alameda Naval Air Base, Joy became a metalsmith. She learned to use different tools and operate machinery, and she was excited about having a job that she was good at. Before the war, Yulan Liu had worked ten hours a day, seven days a week, in a laundry. "There was nothing heavier than the iron," she said, "Sometimes my arm was so sore at night that I could not hold my chopsticks." "The welding torch," as she remembered, "was lighter," especially since she did not have to hold it for as many hours. She was able to work in different areas on the ships, and she often chatted with people between assignments. Luella Louie, hired as a riveter, also drilled, welded, and operated machinery at the Alameda Naval Air Base after two weeks of training. Ah Yoke Gee no longer sewed late at night. She worked eight hours a day, six days a week, and took Sundays off. . . .

Chinese women were more readily accepted in defense companies than their men. The women had been hired to solve the manpower shortage and to meet the demands of defense production during the war. As thousands of Rosies[4] worked at men's jobs, the news media opened a public debate on gender differences, women's morale, and social order that effectively set female workers apart from their male counterparts. It was understood that black, white, or Chinese women were employed not to replace men but to release them for the cause of Democracy, and would not threaten skilled labor once the war was over. . . .

Overcoming Stereotypes

Because racial stereotypes were still a major obstacle to the integration of the Chinese into U.S. society, Chinese

4. "Rosies" refers to "Rosie the Riveter," a nickname for women who worked in the defense industry during World War II.

American women realized that their performance at work would have a direct impact on the status of all Chinese Americans. The images of Chinese immigrants presented by the media had played an important role in shaping public sentiment against the Chinese in the late nineteenth and early twentieth centuries. Many Chinese American women who engaged in defense work and military service believed that they had the responsibility to educate the general public, and they used their workplace—their access to the larger world—to showcase the strengths of Chinese tradition and culture and prove the intelligence and industriousness of Chinese people. . . .

Changing Gender Roles

The daughters of Chinese American immigrants were quite aware that they were less privileged than their brothers. Many Chinese immigrants expected to live with their sons and grandchildren in the future, so they were more willing to give financial support to their male than to their female offspring. All the children in Elizabeth Lew's family worked when they were young. The girls sewed, and the boys shined shoes and delivered lottery tickets. While Elizabeth and her sitters had to give their parents all the money they made to cover household expenses, the brothers kept their money so that they could afford wives in the future. Similarly, Ah Yoke Gee was an open-minded woman, but when money became tight, Maggie Gee and her sisters knew that only their brothers would be given family money for college.

Chinese women's roles in the community were also limited compared with those of men. Women's hourly wages were usually lower than men's, so they often worked longer hours. Gender lines could also be found in community organizations and activities. Women had no voting rights in the Chinese Consolidated Benevolent Associations, district associations, or family associations. Men made the major decisions, while women were mostly involved in social gatherings, fund-raising, and Red Cross work.

The Chinese community press was cautious in dealing with the issue of women's wartime employment. Chinese American men were more likely to be encouraged to join the army or do defense work; Chinese women's primary roles were still defined by the press as those of wives and mothers. Not one article or editorial in Chinese newspapers specifically called on Chinese women to enter the defense industry. Women's organizations and social clubs were active in roles more readily recognized and praised by the community. "It is the servicemen who will do the fighting for us," C.T. Feng, chairman of the American Women's Voluntary Service, told Chinese American women. "We must show our fighting men that we are absolutely behind them." As part of its war effort, the Chinatown branch of the YWCA in San Francisco started a weekly class to teach women time-saving ways of preparing food. At a YWCA open house meeting, the Y's administrator, Mrs. Jane Kwong Lee, called upon Chinese American women to support the country by giving their families the "right nutritional food."

Chinese American women did not need the approval of the community to respond to the nation's call for defense work and military service, however. They wanted to serve their country, and they wanted to demonstrate that they could do more than get married, have children, and work at women's jobs. They thought it was time for people to view women in a different light. . . .

Ironically, it was through their wartime experience that Chinese women learned that gender inequality was more than a Chinese tradition. In the defense industries women worked as welders, burners, riveters, and machinists, but as the historian Mary Ryan points out, "rather than a genuine alteration in the rules of gender, the admission of women to the male job sector was regarded as an emergency measure, permissible 'for the duration only.'" Women were recruited to provide temporary help in a place where they did not belong. . . .

After the War

Toward the end of the war, the defense industry gradually reduced the volume of production, and the employees were free to leave their jobs. Jade Snow Wong was among those Chinese women who left right away, while Ah Yoke Gee and others stayed on. By the end of 1945, however, most of the nation's defense plants had either converted to conventional production or shut down. Thousands of workers were laid off. With no support from society and limited skills, few American women were able to compete with male workers for industrial jobs. In the San Francisco Bay Area, only the Alameda Naval Air Base let a few women keep their jobs. Marinship, all four Kaiser Richmond shipyards, and most of the other defense companies eventually disappeared.

The war, however, had changed the lives of many Chinese American men and women. Although the majority of white middle-class American women returned to domesticity, most Chinese American women continued to work, but they no longer relied on employment within their own communities. Lanfang Wong, a metalsmith during the war, landed a new job at an insurance company in San Francisco. She later married a war veteran and moved to Napa Valley to work on a farm. After her yard was shut down, Ah Yoke Gee found a job at a post office in Berkeley. Because the Alameda Naval Air Base continued to manufacture defense products in the postwar years, Joy Yee was able to keep her job until 1955, when she gave birth to her first child. She went back to work at the base in 1968 and remained for another seventeen years. To celebrate the fiftieth anniversary of the war, she helped organize a reunion of all the base's Chinese Rosies. Although Elizabeth Lew Anderson had spent years in different parts of the country and overseas because of her husband's job, she was able to go back to her job at the base during the Korean War and the Vietnam War while she was living in the Bay Area. Yuk Wah Fu, also a base employee, kept her job until 1947, when she married. She later worked for the Pacific Bell Company. Aimei Chen left Stockton's Chinatown and settled down in Berkeley. While her husband studied engineering at the University of California under the G.I. Bill, she worked as an office clerk. Yulan Liu left Oakland's Chinatown and became a nursing aide in Vallejo after her husband found work at the Mare Island Naval Shipyard. Lili Wang, who had worked in a Richmond shipyard during the war, began medical school in 1946 and eventually practiced as a physician in Washington, D.C.

Fleeing Communist China for America

Betty Chu

Betty Chu grew up in a wealthy Shanghai family, but she
was working as a secretary in San Francisco when she told
her story to Joan Morrison and Charlotte Fox Zabusky. In
this excerpt from their book of interviews with immigrants, *American Mosaic*, Chu explains that during her
adolescence, the Chinese Communists defeated the Nationalist Party in 1949 after a bitter civil war and established the People's Republic of China. Chu became a
teacher, married, and had a child. At the same time, she
reports, the Communist government began pressuring citizens to conform to Communist thinking and to anti-
Americanism, prompting Chu and her husband to leave
China. He left first, going to Hong Kong on the pretext of
visiting his brother. Chu and her son were eventually permitted to "visit" her husband. They never returned to
Shanghai. After three years in Hong Kong, Chu and her
family immigrated to America.

My grandfather was the head of the family. He was a very
wealthy man. He was a shipowner, and he owned all these
silk stores. My father was some kind of bank officer, but
it wasn't really the source of income. I remember my early
childhood as living in a huge mansion in Shanghai, with
lots of servants, gardeners, chauffeurs, you name it. And
all the old-fashioned cars: DeSoto, Nash, Packard.

It was the fashionable thing when I was born for the

Betty Chu, in *American Mosaic: The Immigrant Experience in the Words of Those
Who Lived It*, edited by Joan Morrison and Charlotte Fox Zabusky. New York: E.P. Dutton, 1980. Copyright © 1980 by Joan Morrison and Charlotte Fox Zabusky. Reproduce
by permission of the publisher.

upper-class people to have Westernized atmosphere. My grandfather had a Westernized reception room, with a huge chandelier, where he would receive his foreign friends. And we had tennis courts in our backyard and a lot of Westernized things.

During my childhood and all those years that I lived in such luxury, I did see a lot of things that are very unfair, even to a child—the extreme difference between the rich and the poor. The servants that we had, they had to learn their manners in order to work in such a mansion, and they have to dress properly. But they all came from very poor rural families. They are allowed to go back to their home to visit maybe once a year, and they bring home any kind of garbage you throw out, because to them it was precious. . . .

Communist Revolution

During my adolescent years the big change took place [the success of the Communist revolution in China]. My grandfather passed away by then, and everybody was saying how really fortunate he was that he didn't have to live to see all these things—to see what he created. . . . We were all terrified, because we understood the people who were going to take over the whole country is going to be—well, the way we put it—like our enemies. This was in 1949.

For myself I was more frightened then about the unknown than what it was really all about. After the Communists took over, the first few years, they were very lenient—meaning they tolerated a lot of things that we thought are going to be normal. I remember very clearly. I was in my early teens, so I really cared more about Frank Sinatra records than the real political scene. I guess to me it was a very important thing, and also boyfriends and parties and so forth. And they tolerated all those. . . .

Well, things began to change and we felt ropes tightening up around our necks. It was about the Korean War time. A lot of really big things were going on, such as the reforms of the businessmen. But to a teen-age person, as long as they didn't directly affect the family, I didn't pay too much attention. It was kind of remote, just like the Japanese occupation.[1]

Then the government started banning anything that's American, and they started what we would call brainwashing. They started all this propaganda about the worst enemy of the Chinese people were the United States of America and the people. Everything pertaining to the U.S. is just crime, sin, bad, stinks. So we just thought that for the sake of survival we'd just better go along with them and destroy or hide all our things that's American. I had to get rid of my records. It was heartbreaking. . . .

Political Study

After I got married—my husband used to work for a bank at that time—we had to think about our financial aspects as a family. So I thought maybe I'd better start looking for a job. Now, people don't just look for jobs. In order to get work, I had to go through this training. That was really something. They needed teachers very much, and they were telling the whole world that they are going to educate the people. It sounded good, really. So I went through this short training program, and I was a high-school teacher, assigned arithmetic, geometry, algebra, and the rest is political study. . . .

There were all these movements. They always had a different topic, such as cultural revolution and anti-Confucius and so on. Then we witnessed what they called "the struggling"—meaning one individual in the middle of a room full of maybe two hundred people, and you struggle him. You're not supposed to physically struggle him, but after

1. Japan invaded and occupied China from 1937 to 1945.

a while people's emotions got out of hand. . . .

They're not supposed to physically attack the person. They can just ask him all kinds of questions. Ask questions—that's not putting it really correctly. They would say, "You're not telling enough. Come on and tell us. Otherwise you're going to. . . ." And they'd make all kinds of threats. That's how people got to live in fear.

The way I felt, it was all fixed. If the group wants to get so-and-so into trouble, then he's got it. People got frightened, because nobody likes to be the object. The final result, after months of harassment—you either got sent to some remote provinces, or anyway it was nothing good, nothing pleasant.

Due to the fact that I was a teacher in a showcase school, my boy was fortunate enough to be one out of millions to be allowed into that showcase nursery school. They were teaching the youngsters propaganda about American people. "America and American people are the worst enemies of our country" went on and on until the Soviet Union was number-one enemy on the list.

When my son brought home all this educational information, he was so frightened. He'd come home only on weekends, you see—that gives us people a chance to devote our whole self to work for the people. So he came home one weekend, and the poor little thing—he was just shivering and he had tears in his eyes, and he told me, "I know how the American people look like." I discovered later on, when I paid that nursery school a visit, it was a poster of a green-faced, very ugly-looking Uncle Sam, with his tall hat and his long, monsterlike fingernails. You know what the nursery-school teacher actually told the kids at that nursery-school age? She told them, "You know what the American people's favorite food is?" And the little kids were already trembling like leaves, and she said, "Little children's hearts." I thought that was very, very wrong.

The Decision to Leave

That and some similar events led me to the secret—of course it had to be a very secret—decision that we have to leave. My husband and I secretly discussed it in the middle of the night; we felt safe between the two of us in the middle of the night. We finally decided maybe we can take a big chance by letting my husband apply for the permit for us, because there is no such thing as the whole family applying. People don't have the courage to apply, because that exposes your intention, which means you are putting yourself on the opposite side of the people. You're an enemy right away. They never would admit that you could not leave the country, but the thing is you just cannot. . . .

So he left, just to Hong Kong. He only asked for a month, but everybody knew that it was just a laugh. He was trying to work and wait for us to get out. My superior knew about my husband's movement, and of course right away my whole status changed. Not that I still want to be in their favor anymore. But after that their attitude toward me . . . [*sighs*] . . . especially my little boy. He was going to nursery school at that time. The words get around in the neighborhood, so people knew his father was in Hong Kong. That put him in a bad spot, the poor kid. He came home, not really bruised but red-eyed, and he kept telling me secretly, without letting anybody else hear him, that people are just hitting him—little kids hitting him, pushing him around, and calling him "son of a Hong Kong spy." He asks, "Is my father a Hong Kong spy?" So then things went from bad to worse. It was very uncomfortable. . . .

So I applied for a permit to visit my husband. You have to go through all kinds of humiliation. They laugh at you, scorn you, verbally abuse. In order to get what I wanted, the permit, I didn't mind what they said to me, what they did to me. I gave them all kinds of reasons—anything, everything. Six times I was rejected. [*Laughs softly.*] I can laugh now, but think of the tears I shed. By then my boy was a student, and pretty soon he would be wearing one of those red scarves to be a member of the Pioneer, and after that the next step is a member of the Youth Group, and after that the next step is a member of the [Communist] Party—because otherwise you never make any good. You won't get a chance to go even to junior high school. . . . I just didn't want that kind of fate for my son. So I tried and I tried and I tried.

Permitted to Leave China

Then I was really frantic, because when the boy gets to be a certain age, he cannot be included in my permit anymore. And there was things that I heard about—like a mother and a child applied for a permit and they will give one a permit and none to the other. What are you going to do? Leave the child back? Finally, I got to pray a lot—all in secret, never in the open. I left the whole thing to the Lord. I just let the Lord decide whether I should leave the country and join my husband or not. I got hold of a dusty old Bible, and I said, "I don't remember my English anymore, but I'll read the Bible." So I prayed. And after the sixth rejection, the seventh time I was granted a permit.

I only applied for a month. They told me casually to mail back my permit. "And be sure to leave your rationing cards behind for rice and so forth. And what are you going to do with your apartment, now that you are going?" I said, "Oh, I have to keep it for when I come back." "Oh, when you come back, we'll get you someplace to live," knowing all the time that everybody's lying to each other. I said, "Well, whatever the government thinks I should do." The government would think you should give the apartment back, so they can give it to someone else.

We went to Hong Kong to join my husband. He was doing pretty good. He started from the very bottom, of course, and he was working his way up. It was a very big adjustment for both myself and my son. We had to adjust to everything else outside, and we also had to adjust to my husband, to living with him.

We stayed in Hong Kong a little over three years. I guess three years changed a lot of our attitudes for us. It took only a few Western movies to change my son's whole attitude toward the American people.

Things began to happen. They started to have bomb threats, and a lot of stores were changing their flags. The Communists took over Macao, and we thought Hong Kong was threatened. So that made us make up our mind, just like that. We said, "If it took us all that trouble to get out of the country to go to Hong Kong, *if* there is the remotest chance of their taking over Hong Kong, we're going to leave." My husband had worked nearly to the top of his organization, but he was willing to give up all of that. He was making a very good salary, high position, we had servants, but. . . . We had our little girl by then, and thinking of the future of the children, we don't want anything like what we experienced ever to happen to them. That's why we were really willing to give up all that. And my husband's brother here in this country [the United States] was saying, "If you want to come over to this country, we'll sponsor." He came as a student, twenty years ago. We came as immigrants in 1969.

The FBI came to visit me after we arrived. It was a friendly visit. I was a little disappointed, because the man was very nice and friendly. He was sitting there just like a friend. First, he showed you the badges, like they do in the movies. Now, in China, they have authority to walk in, and nobody dare asks anybody to show anything. You better tell them everything or you're in trouble. But here, the man was very courteous. I guess at first I was a little bit tense, but he put me to ease and he was chatting like an old friend. He even said in case there is any trouble of any kind, I can call him. I had the phone number and the name of an FBI agent. I was very proud.

He did ask me some things, like, did I hear from my brother in China lately, and am I writing letters to him. I thought, "You would know before me anyway," so I told the truth: "No, I wasn't communicating with them." And I think he asked me if there's anyone that I know who came out of the country recently. I told him all the truth that I knew, and it apparently wasn't that interesting. [*Laughs.*]

My son is in high school now. With him it was one big adjustment right after the other. He had to learn the different dialect in Hong Kong, and then he had to learn American here. I don't know how the guy went through it, but he never stopped behind in his class. I don't know how he did it. I just don't know how he did it. He's always been a quiet boy. He just doesn't have that many friends. It does still worry me. [*Sighs.*]

One of my son's biggest disappointments is that my daughter doesn't speak Chinese. Well, she was a year and a half when she came over, and she thought she was American all along. Now she wants to grow up to be an Italian.

Last year, December, we became citizens. The doctor at the hospital where I work invited us over for a party. He surprised us by standing up and announcing it. He said, "Something very wonderful happened last week," and told everybody that we were citizens now. He gave us an American flag as a present, and everybody drank to us. It was very heartwarming.

The Successes and Troubles of High-Tech Immigrants

Iris Chang

When the Chinese Exclusion Act of 1882 was overturned in 1943, a quota system was established that set the number of Chinese immigrants allowed into the United States at 105 persons per year. Further reforms in the immigration law in 1965 and 1990 allowed greater numbers of Asian immigrants, especially highly educated workers, into the United States. Journalist Iris Chang reviews the opportunities that immigration reforms and high-technology employment provided to Chinese immigrants in her book *The Chinese in America*, from which the following selection was excerpted. Some immigrants, such as Jerry Yang, one of the founders of Yahoo!, became wildly successful, but others were treated like "high-tech slaves" by employers and exploited under the threat of visa revocation. Chang also discusses the persistent undercurrent of suspicion directed toward many Chinese immigrants during this period. When the Soviet Union dissolved, China became America's major Cold War rival, and Americans' fear of Chinese espionage extended to Chinese Americans. According to Chang, the prime example of this race-based suspicion is the case of Chinese American scientist Wen Ho Lee, who was accused in 1999 of passing secrets to the Chinese government. He was cleared of espionage and received an apology from the judge in the case. Chang is the author of *The Rape of Nanking* and *Thread of the Silkworm*.

For "high-tech" Chinese, the 1990s resembled the gold rush days, except that the 1990 fortune seekers were mining for nuggets in a new form of sand—silicon. The modern gold rush, like the 1849 gold rush, occurred in northern California, but this time south of San Francisco, in a region dubbed Silicon Valley. The area had already witnessed the birth of the personal computer revolution in the 1970s, when two young men, Steve Jobs and Steve Wozniak, started the Apple corporation, selling desktop computers they had built in their garage. Proximity to Stanford University in Palo Alto, the University of California at Berkeley, and San Francisco as a major port for trade with Asia, helped transform the area into a world center of the high-tech industry. But an even bigger revolution erupted in the 1990s—the Internet revolution. . . .

Internet Searches and Semiconductors

One icon of the dotcom world was Jerry Yang, the billionaire founder of Yahoo!, an Internet search engine and Web service. Born in Taiwan in 1967, Yang moved with his family to San Jose, California, while he was still a teenager. His company grew out of a simple idea: to create a directory of his favorite sites on the international network of information now referred to as the World Wide Web. By the early 1990s, any location on the Web could be accessed by typing the location's Web address into an address box. Yang helped develop the first popular search tool for the Web, so that users could type names or relevant phrases into a search box, and have the search engine find all documents with a string of characters matching those in the search box. In a tiny office trailer at Stanford University, Yang, then a twenty-six-year-old doctoral student in electrical engineering, and his classmate, David Filo, sorted hyperlinks by subject and posted them on the Web. Their directory grew so popular that its level of traffic crashed the computer servers at Stanford, forcing the company to move off campus. Yang and Filo took Yahoo! public and watched its worth increase exponentially as the Internet market exploded. By March 2000, the market capitalization of Yahoo! had exceeded $100 billion.

Of course, not all Chinese moguls of the information age made their wealth through dotcom firms. Some, like Morris Chang, earned their fortunes by enabling high-tech companies to outsource their manufacturing to Taiwan. Revered as the "godfather of high technology" in Taiwan, Chang, an electrical engineer educated at Harvard, MIT, and Stanford, pioneered the integrated circuit foundry industry as the founder and chairman of Taiwan Semiconductor Manufacturing Corporation (TSMC). Recognizing that fabricating chips required enormous startup capital (a semiconductor factory could cost literally billions of dollars), Chang's company, largely funded by the government of the Republic of China in Taiwan, permitted small American chip companies to contract their fabrication work in Taiwan. Taiwan Semiconductor provided independent chip designers, who could not compete on their own against giants like Intel, Motorola, and NEC, access to affordable manufacturing services, freeing them to focus on creative design work. Thus Chang's insight accelerated the pace of computer innovation worldwide. Thousands of entrepreneurs were now able to compete by offering their own innovations, instead of leaving the industry's development to just a few corporate players. By the end of the twentieth century, even colossal semiconductor companies began cutting costs by farming out their fabrication work to Taiwan.

The H1-B Visa Program

Any gold rush has a few celebrity winners and many exhausted losers. Some Chinese immigrants found themselves in a quandary when Congress passed the Immigration Act of 1990, introducing the H1-B visa program for highly educated and skilled immigrant workers, but restricting the time such visa holders could work in the United States to a maximum of six years. The act abruptly reversed previous immigration policy, which had eagerly welcomed foreign immigrants with advanced education or professional occupations. After 1965, the government had imposed virtually no limits on the admission of Chinese foreign nationals with specialized training. In 1989, the foreign Chinese students who happened to be in the United States during the Tiananmen Square massacre were allowed to obtain green cards immediately. But for those who came after the 1990 act, it was a different story.

High-tech employers viewed the H1-B program as an attractive solution to their labor needs because it gave them a fresh crop of minds to exploit every six years. The policy was perceived as giving domestic industry the opportunity to harness the brainpower of foreign immigrants, but without granting these contributors the full rights and privileges of American citizenship. At first, Congress capped the program at 65,000 visas per year, but the 1990s high-tech boom created a massive shortage of computer programmers, engineers, and systems analysts, which companies hoped to rectify by recruiting from abroad. After intense lobbying from corporations like Microsoft, the U.S. government raised the cap on H1-B visas to 115,000 in 1998, then to 195,000 two years later. India provided the greatest number of skilled foreign workers in the program, followed by the People's Republic of China [PRC].

Critics soon denounced the H1-B visa program as "white-collar indentured servitude." Middlemen recruiters took as much as half the salary of the workers they procured for companies, and visa holders were beholden to their employers, whom they needed as sponsors for permanent immigration status. If an H1-B visa holder wanted to switch companies, the potential new employer had to petition the Immigration and Naturalization Service [INS], a process that could take several months. Those with H1-B visas had to wait years for a coveted green card, knowing that their visas might expire before they obtained one. Severe backlogs for green card applications developed because applicants from any one country could not make up more than 7 percent of the total number of green cards issued each year.

By the end of the decade, a few Chinese H1-B visa holders had begun to organize. In 1998, for example, Swallow Yan, a green card applicant from the PRC, helped create the Immigration Council of the Chinese Professionals and Entrepreneurs Association, a grassroots effort that lobbies politicians on behalf of H1-B visa holders. But in general, most H1-B visa holders were too terrified to voice their complaints to the press or lawmakers. While researching this book, I interviewed several Chinese on H1-B visas who spoke to me only on condition of anonymity.

One woman, whom I will call Sally Chung, asserted that the H1-B visa program had turned her into "a high-tech slave." An immigrant from mainland China, she came to the United States in 1992 to obtain a bachelor's degree in engineering. After graduation, she accepted a position as a software designer at a local company, where she was expected to work at least ten hours a day, including weekends, without raises or compensation for overtime. Though Chung was unhappy with her situation, she could not afford to leave—her application for a green card depended on being employed by this particular company. Quitting her job meant starting the paperwork all over again as well as forfeiting the $10,000 she had invested in legal fees for the green card. A backlog at INS caused the wait to stretch from months to several agonizing years. When she complained that she earned even less than entry-level workers in her field, her boss demoted her title from software engineer to librarian in order to justify her low wages. At the same time, however, he expected her to serve as a software engineer by programming a computer database for the company. "My boss enjoys calling me into his office, shutting the door, and then screaming at me," she said. "He tells me I have to speak perfect English without an accent before I can get a raise. He says that if he lived in China for only one month, he would be able to speak perfect Chinese. My boss warned me that if I ask him for a raise one more time he will fire me." Now, she says, "I'm scared to death I'll lose my job."

U.S.-China Relations

In addition to the H1-B visa system, another development worked against the interests of the "high-tech" Chinese. The sudden demise of the Soviet Union left a vacuum in the arena of international politics, helping China emerge from the cold war as the second greatest military power in the world after the United States. While the economies of Russia and the former Soviet republics were still paying the price for the arms race the Soviet Union could not afford, the economy of the People's Republic of China was growing almost exponentially. After Mao's [Mao Zedong, leader of Communist China] death, the Chinese gross national product had almost tripled by the 1990s, giving rise to American fears of future competition. During the 1990s, economic experts and historians predicted that the next century would belong to mainland China.

One irony of the 1990s was that the United States would come to view China both as its great business partner and its most powerful rival. While the decade saw an explosion of Sino-American corporate partnerships, it also witnessed the dawn of a new era of suspicion regarding the People's

Republic. The *Washington Post* reported the emergence of an anti-PRC "Blue Team" in Washington, D.C., "a loose alliance of members of Congress, congressional staff, think tank fellows, Republican political operatives, conservative journalists, lobbyists for Taiwan, former intelligence officers and a handful of academics, all united in the view that a rising China poses great risks to America's vital interests." A spate of books published in the late 1990s or shortly afterward by members of this Blue Team—*The Coming Conflict with China*, by Richard Bernstein and Ross Munro; *Hegemon: China's Plan to Dominate Asia and the World*, by Steven W. Mosher; *The China Threat: How the People's Republic Targets America*, by Bill Gertz; *Year of the Rat* and *Red Dragon Rising: Communist China's Military Threat to America*, by Edward Timperlak and William Triplett—suggested that a future showdown between the United States and the PRC was inevitable, echoing earlier cold war themes with only the name of the enemy changed.

In 1999, Representative Christopher Cox (R-Calif.) released a seven-hundred-page report accusing mainland China of stealing classified data on American nuclear weapons. Although the report was later denounced by American scientists and missile experts as grossly distorted and erroneous, it received enormous media attention upon its release. In an initial response, *Time* magazine published a cover story about the possibility of the United States entering a new cold war, this time with China.

Scrutiny of Ethnic Chinese

With this atmosphere of suspicion came greater scrutiny of ethnic Chinese scientists and engineers, greater fears that they might be potential spies. Historically, the fate of the Chinese American community has always been linked to the health of Sino-American relations, and the 1990s were no exception. Like Tsien Hsue-shen and other Chinese victims of the McCarthy era[1] of the 1950s, Chinese intellectuals who worked in national defense in the 1990s found themselves suspected of espionage because of their racial heritage and their great number within the high-tech industry.

In 1992, the NASA Ames Research Center fired Raymond Luh, an aerospace engineer and immigrant from Taiwan for possessing "a paper with Chinese writing on it." The following year, a court order confined Andrew Wang, a computer scientist, to his Denver home for almost a year after he e-mailed computer code to a friend in town. Wang's employer had accused him of stealing the code to start a business with alleged Chinese financing. The FBI wanted to pursue the matter as an interstate crime—because Wang's e-mail had been routed through the Internet by a switching system outside of Colorado—but the authorities later dropped the charges when they learned that Wang's boss had given him permission to copy the information and that none of it was particularly important. David Lane, Wang's attorney, attributed the entire matter to a "yellow high-tech peril" kind of fear, adding that his client's life had been "virtually ruined" for more than a year.

Émigrés, even those reared and educated in Nationalist-controlled Taiwan, were soon being accused of passing information to Communist China. The new climate of suspicion prompted people to come out of the closet and speak frankly about their past treatment by the U.S. government. In 1982, Dr. Chih-Ming Hu had received an unexpected visit from an FBI agent. At the time, Hu, a graduate of National Taiwan University with a doctorate from the University of Maryland, was working on a nonclassi-

1. Senator Joseph McCarthy actively attempted to expose American Communists.

fied flight simulation project at Computer Sciences Corporation, a contractor for NASA Ames in Mountain View, California. The FBI agent asked Hu if he had ever given classified secrets and his doctoral dissertation to a friend in mainland China. No, Hu said, adding that he had no access to classified data and that his dissertation was already in the public domain, having been published in the *Journal of Chemical Physics*. A few days later, the agent reappeared, this time accusing Hu of lying and threatening to have him fired by NASA. Vehemently, Hu insisted he was telling the truth and even offered to take a polygraph test. The agent, who did not take up his offer, warned Hu that he suspected him of hiding something. A week later, NASA fired Hu for security reasons, even though he was never officially charged with anything. . . .

The Case of Wen Ho Lee

The most notorious case of unjustified treatment involved Dr. Wen Ho Lee, a Taiwanese American scientist at the Los Alamos National Laboratory in New Mexico. In March 1999, a *New York Times* article claimed that Los Alamos was the source of the W-88 nuclear warhead technology that the People's Republic of China was believed to have obtained through espionage. Lee was abruptly fired without a hearing, and that December, authorities indicted him for allegedly transferring nuclear secrets from a classified computer network onto an insecure computer, and then onto ten portable tapes, seven of which were missing. FBI agents immediately arrested Lee and charged him with fifty-nine counts of mishandling sensitive information and secrecy violations of the Atomic Energy Act.

After a comprehensive three-year investigation involving more than 260 agents and a thousand interviews, during which time Lee was held in custody, under especially dreadful conditions, the United States Justice Department conceded it had no evidence that Lee had committed espionage. The U.S. government also admitted the embarrassing fact that they either knew, or should have learned early in the investigation, that the secret information in the design of the W-88 warhead in Beijing's possession could not have come from Los Alamos. What China had was based not on the early-stage design used in Los Alamos, but a later-stage version distributed to at least 548 addresses within the U.S. government, available to hundreds if not thousands of people across America.

While many details of the Wen Ho Lee case remain classified, what has emerged is a pattern of government incompetence and outright misconduct. During an interrogation conducted on March 7, 1999, federal agents tried to coerce Dr. Lee to confess to espionage, resorting even to death threats. The FBI told him that he had failed his polygraph, when in fact he had passed it with flying colors. They hinted at the power of the government to manipulate the media by leaking information, and the power of the subsequent coverage to destroy his career and ruin his life, even if he were completely innocent. Agents even warned Lee that he could be executed if he did not cop to a lesser plea and confess. "Do you know who the Rosenbergs are?" FBI agent Carol Covert asked Lee. "The Rosenbergs are the only people that never cooperated with the federal government in an espionage case. You know what happened to them? They electrocuted them, Wen Ho."

When the Justice Department could find no evidence that Lee had spied for Beijing, they changed focus, seizing upon the fact that he had improperly handled data within Los Alamos National Laboratory. Lee later admitted that he had moved nuclear codes from a secure computer system to an insecure computer within the laboratory, but claimed he did it only as backup, to protect his files in the event of a system failure. . . .

According to Lee's colleagues, such security lapses were common, and the data Lee had downloaded fell in a gray area of classification: "protect as restricted data," or PARD. This meant the data had to be handled with care, as it might contain sensitive information, but did not merit the same kind of security precautions as "secret" or even "confidential" data. Scientists could leave PARD on their desks overnight, and a former weapons designer at Los Alamos admitted to the *Times* that he had committed his own blunder with PARD when the wind blew a sheaf of documents out a window. But after Lee's arrest, the U.S. government reclassified the downloaded PARD files to a much higher level—as "secret restricted data"—a decision critics described as politically motivated, an attempt to justify what had already been done to Lee. . . .

In the fall of 2000, to salvage a rapidly eroding case against Lee, the Justice Department worked out a plea bargain with his attorneys, dropping all but one of the fifty-nine counts in exchange for his agreement to cooperate with federal authorities. The judge later apologized to Lee, asserting that he had been "terribly wronged" and admitting that federal prosecutors had "embarrassed our entire nation." It was later discovered that several government leaks to the media were not only lies but also violations of U.S. law. The following year, declassified portions of an eight-hundred-page report commissioned by Attorney General Janet Reno concluded that "the FBI has been investigating a crime which was never established to have occurred."

The incident left a lasting wound on the psyche of the Chinese American community. They would remember not only the unbounded arrogance of the Justice Department but also the role of an irresponsible press that fanned flames of racist paranoia across America. During the Lee investigation, the media exploited cruel caricatures of the

Chinese, reminding historians of the racist cartoons that led to the exclusion era of the nineteenth century.[2]. . .

Wake-Up Call

The Wen Ho Lee case served as wake-up call for the Chinese at the national laboratories. The case and its aftermath forced many Chinese American scientists—particularly those in the second wave—to rethink their priorities. Why devote their energies to supporting institutions that regarded them as untrustworthy? Would their talents not be better served in a more respectful environment? If the U.S. government did not reward their effort, or withheld promotions on the basis of skin color and ethnicity, then why did it deserve the best years of their lives? They began to complain of an environment rife with nepotism, incompetence, and racial prejudice, all of which deprived Chinese Americans of recognition. Joel Wong, an immigrant engineer at Lawrence Livermore National Laboratory in California, spoke for thousands of other Chinese Americans in *Science* magazine: "The term going around now among us is that we're high-tech coolies—if we work hard, we're given more work." He and other Asian Americans, several of them Taiwanese American, charged that a glass ceiling kept them from the ranks of upper management. They called the performance evaluations "subjective, arbitrary and capricious" because they were conducted in secret, were hard to contest, and were influenced by the "old-boys network.". . .

Many Chinese immigrant scientists had originally entered the labs because they appeared to offer not only an intellectual environment, but also the secure haven that had eluded their early years. As immigrants who had fled war and revolution since childhood, many longed for a cer-

2. Most Chinese immigrants were denied entry into the United States under the Chinese Exclusion Act of 1882.

tain measure of peace and stability. Now they began to wonder about their decision. "In hindsight, there are some things I might have done differently," Wen Ho Lee later wrote. "I might have made different career decisions, maybe going to work in private industry, or teaching at a university, rather than devoting more than twenty years to the national laboratories."

A Visit to China

Ben Fong-Torres

In this selection from his book on growing up Chinese American, *The Rice Room*, Ben Fong-Torres describes a trip he took to China in 1982 with a group of American entertainers. On this trip Fong-Torres, a Californian, took the opportunity to visit his immigrant parents' home villages in southern China. He describes meeting many of his relatives for the first time and his appreciation for his family and heritage. At the same time, Fong-Torres sees firsthand the poverty and daily struggle for existence, and he states that he understands in a deeper way why his parents emigrated from China in order to find a better life in America. Fong-Torres has written for dozens of magazines, including *Rolling Stone*, *GQ*, and *Esquire*, and written and edited several anthologies. His books include *Not Fade Away* and *The Hits Just Keep on Coming*.

For me, China was crystallized into one day: our fourth day in the country.

It was a Monday in mid-March. Our troupe was in a little town called Shigi, and, out on my own, I found myself admiring a tray of *don tot* when I was interrupted. *Don tot*—custard tarts—are a staple of *dim sum* trays these days, but for me, these particular tarts were nostalgic. I had first seen such tarts in China in 1948, when I was three.

Now, in 1982, I was back, and people were gawking. My skin may be yellow, but to the townspeople of Shigi, I was clearly not Chinese. They didn't need to note my latter-

Ben Fong-Torres, *The Rice Room: Growing Up Chinese-American—from Number Two Son to Rock'n'Roll*. New York: Hyperion, 1994. Copyright © 1994 by Ben Fong-Torres. Reproduced by permission of the publisher.

day Beatles bowl haircut or my Nike sportswear to make that judgment. They could tell by my *posture* that I was a Westerner.

I stood there, gazing longingly at these pieces of pastry, when two women approached and offered to buy me one. I was stunned. In the three days I'd been in China, I'd become accustomed to being treated by strangers like some relative who'd gone astray. But now I had been challenged, obligated to respond in kind. That is, in Cantonese. "No, thank you very much," I said, in *tze-yup*. By refusing, I had done the proper thing. But instead of insisting—which is the next proper thing—the two women let out roaring laughs that stopped just short of harshness. They knew exactly where my parents were from, one of them said. They could tell by the way I spoke.

I was in luck. I had hoped to take a side trip from Shigi to find my parents' ancestral villages—in the Hoi Ping region, not far from where we were, according to my maps. The women weren't sure, but they read the name of the village on the back of a photo my father had given me of his brother. They consulted a couple of bystanders who were watching us. One of them said the village was close enough to get to by car, and pointed to a shack across the street. A small sign, in English, read: CARS FOR HIRE.

I tried to express my thanks again, and they laughed again. "Go home," one of the women said, in the dialect that I heard as an echo of my own. "Go home."

Gifts for the Family

I asked Sero, a Hong Kong woman who was a production assistant on the show [*Cycling Through China*], to accompany me and help interpret. At our hotel, the head clerk on our floor told me what to bring.

"Buy a chicken and some pork," she said. At stores, she instructed, I should ask for candy—*lop jook*—and incense—*tong shuen*. I'd need red paper for the money I'd give out. How much? "A few dollars—doesn't matter, as long as the bills are clean." She reminded me how rarely Chinese people got to travel.

"Three hours away," she said. "That's *far!*"

At 8:20 the next morning, Sero and I met our driver and loaded my gifts into the trunk. Soon after she gave him instructions, our blue Toyota was hurtling out of town and over what passed for highways. We rolled past straw-hatted peasants and teams of water buffalo working the rice paddies and farmlands all along the way. Technology had been slow coming to China, and the land was worked the way it always had been.

We hit a stretch of road lined with tall trees, and for a brief moment, I felt as if I was in Beverly Hills, until, beyond the trees, I could see streams and farmland, and I was back amidst the communes of China. Our taxi clambered onto a ferry to cross several tributaries and rivers on the way to Chek Hom. Wherever we were, we saw people at work; women hauling wooden wagons loaded with baskets of coal; men and women carrying entire garlic trees.

"Look at her," Sero said, pointing out her window to a young woman walking calmly down the road with a load of straw the size of a baby grand piano on her shoulders.

I shook my head in amazement. "In America, two young men probably couldn't lift that," I said.

Sero smiled. "The people here are very healthy," she said.

We overtook bicycles weighed down with crates containing anything from geese to fresh produce. We sped past buses and rumbling minitractors, past construction workers on bamboo scaffolding. Everywhere, it seemed, China was being built.

We stopped briefly in Sun Wi, which happened to be Sero's ancestral village. While she chatted with some of the people, I watched a crew of construction workers in white hard hats taking a break, chewing on *jeh*, sections of sugar canes I remembered Dad giving us at the New Eastern Cafe.

China is a country of basic truths. With Sero by my side, I asked a young woman what she did for a living.

"Work," she replied.

In Mother's Village

As we entered Chek Hom—my mother's village—the portraits my parents had drawn vanished into the dusty air, replaced by actual people, deeply lined and tanned, going about their business in town. Some stood idly around in front of decayed buildings; others hawked goods—*jeh*, peanuts, garlic, greens, and roasted meats—along the streets. At the sight of our car, they all stopped and stared.

Sero turned to me. "Your cousin's going to be a star for a whole month," she said, "between you coming from America and this car."

At our designated meeting spot in town, a young man who introduced himself as my cousin's son greeted us and got in to direct the driver to my aunt's house. Even as we made the final few turns, the cynic in me remembered warnings I'd received, both in San Francisco and here: Overseas Chinese are often mobbed by villagers, counterfeit cousins hopeful of a gift of cash. But with this man, there was no question. When he spoke, I could hear an accent within the dialect, a rhythm of the words that I'd heard all my life. He sounded just like my parents.

I had no idea what to expect. In our few days in China, we had yet to visit a commune, and, on the road to Shigi, I had seen housing only from a distance. The sight was distressing. I remember stately, fortresslike buildings that looked as if they'd survived fires, but even more arresting were the mud huts covered with a mosaic of tar paper and remnants of old clothes.

We stopped on a wide dirt street, and I knew I was in a residential neighborhood. Clothing hung off bamboo racks in front of almost every door and from second-floor balconies. My cousin's son led us to a white, two-story row-house. We entered through a blue metal door and into the dark front room, where a half-dozen people were waiting for me.

Meeting the Family

The Chinese are not a demonstrative people, and it was my cousin—the mother of the young man who had delivered us—who stepped forward to greet me with a handshake, and to introduce me to my other relatives. Her mother was my mother's only sister, a woman who was seventy-four. Her hair gray and thin, she sat in a straight back chair and smiled from behind her eyeglasses, and looked more like *Po-Po*, my grandmother, than *Ma-Ma*.

My cousin also introduced an uncle—Mother's only surviving brother of three—and two in-laws. All in their seventies, they wore single-colored shirts with Chinese collars, slacks, and sandals, while my cousin, in her early forties, wore a bright, patterned, Western-style blouse.

Before long, I had met a dozen relatives, including two babies. It was a blizzard of relations; I lost track immediately, and I was actually grateful when several of them left after exchanging pleasantries. I wanted to absorb as much as I could, to report back to my family, but it seemed improper to whip out a tape recorder or notepad. And so I was what they expected: the good, obedient son of Tui Wing and Kwok Shang, here to visit from *Mai Gok* ["the beautiful country," or America].

I took in the front room with pleasure. I hadn't yet seen the whole house, but there was a vibrancy about this room that indicated that my mother's family—*my* family—was doing all right. The room burst with colors, mainly lucky red and gold, on paper scrolls. I looked, with new appreciation, at prints of Chinese watercolor scenes, the kind I saw on calendars Chinatown banks and merchants handed out, and that my parents hung in every room. A portable stereo system sat atop a cabinet.

As in every Chinese family home, a place of honor was reserved for portraits of deceased elders. On the back wall was a large, framed photograph of my grandmother. It was the same picture I'd seen so often as a child in Oakland. And along a side wall, several long frames held montages of photos, one of them devoted to my immediate family. There we were—in grade school, graduating from high school, getting married—our life histories hanging on a wall in a house in southern China. I looked around at the anxious, smiling faces before me and realized that I had many more cousins than the ones I'd met at all those Chinatown banquets.

Telling About Life in America

Over tea, we talked about family, about life in San Francisco, about our common desires for reunions. "Their letters and those pictures," my cousin said, indicating the wall, "that's how we stay in touch. We look at them every day and think about you."

I told my cousin that it would be wonderful to have them come to America, to see my parents and our family. She and her mother laughed gently at my naiveté. They couldn't even leave the county without going through miles of red tape.

I soon realized that Sero, sitting and sipping tea, didn't have much to do. Every bit of Cantonese I'd ever learned, pitiful scraps that they were, seemed to be coming back.

"Come see the house," my cousin said. I soon realized that the front room was the showcase. Wherever I went, I got the feeling I was in a cave. The kitchen, like most in

China, was open-air. Between the kitchen and front room was a small area set aside for worshipping departed relatives. We came to a stop. "Time to pay respects," she said. She mentioned a few names I didn't know, and, following her lead, I bowed three times. And once more, for [his deceased older brother] Barry.

Upstairs, several simple bunks crowded a bedroom. It looked like a cozy jail cell, but my relatives said they were happy to have this house. And, they added, they had it because we had sent money over the years.

China in the Cultural Revolution

I asked my aunt about life under communism. When the Communists took over, the family lost ownership of its house and its fruit farm. "During the Great Cultural Revolution," she said, "we were not allowed to wear earrings and bracelets. If people saw you wearing them, they would take them from you." A few years ago, she said, the government sent her son and daughter-in-law to another county. "I got ill and there was no one to take care of me. I didn't look like this before. I was fat and strong. I had to stay in bed for two years. This was the only bad thing." She thought a moment, then continued: "And things were scarce. Money had no value. No matter how much money you had, you could not buy anything. That was not good."

Although the fruit farm was still state property, the government had returned the family's house to her. Life, she said, had improved in recent years, again thanks largely to money sent from our family in the United States.

I asked my aunt if she'd wanted to go to the Golden Mountains [a nickname for the United States] years ago. She sighed. "Yes, I would have loved to go. But no one married me and took me over. I was very miserable. If I were able to go, I would have been very happy. I am too old now. There is no more opportunity."

I wanted to locate my father's older brother. Aunt told me that they hadn't seen him in some time. With my cousin accompanying us, we took a short ride, then walked a narrow farmland road into my father's village. It was much smaller than my mother's, the homes all squat, low, brick buildings fronted by dirt yards littered with tree branches and other debris.

In a dark shack, we found my uncle sitting on a rumpled, straw-matted wooden bed, as if he were in solitary confinement. He looked like he'd just been awakened in late afternoon.

So this was my father's birthplace. Dirt floors, mud-brick walls, no windows, no electricity. Now I understood why he slept in the temple, why he escaped to Manila, why he made the journey to the United States.

It took my uncle several moments to comprehend my visit, to grasp the fact that the son of his brother had suddenly materialized. I told him, in my fractured Cantonese, that I was happy to see him and that my father sent his best wishes. I asked if he had a message for him.

He groaned. "Send some money," he managed. Several of his neighbors had gathered at the doorway to look at his visitors, and my cousin spoke with them. She learned that my uncle and aunt had received money from my parents, but he was no longer capable of writing. Still, he needed money for food and medicine.

Whatever I hadn't given to my mother's relatives, I now left with him. I only wished I had more with me, and I felt suddenly guilty for buying some video games in Hongkong. I promised Uncle that I would send more money.

Leaving Home

Back in my mother's village, it was time to say goodbye, and there was no getting around it: Through the long grips of each other's hands, and through the tears of farewell, I didn't feel as if I were leaving *for* home. I was leaving home.

I sat, dazed, in the car, unaware of all the bumps on the way back to Shigi. I had been to where my mother and father came from. This was what they'd been trying to tell us all those years, about how tough they'd had it, and about how lucky we were. All that talk that we'd come to think of, and even dismiss, as clichés.

A few afternoons later, Wenda Fong, one of the show's producers, looked up and down the dirt roads of a small China town and sighed.

"There but for fortune go I," she said. I knew what she meant.

Snakeheads and Smuggling

Peter Kwong

Chinese immigrants to the United States after World War II were mainly refugees from Communist China and those hoping to reunite with families living in America. Highly skilled immigrants destined to work in American high-tech industries also migrated to the United States during this period. However, by the late twentieth and into the twenty-first century, a new group of immigrants began appearing in the Chinatowns of major American cities. Most were from poverty-stricken areas of rural China, seeking a better life, much like those Chinese immigrants who came to America in the nineteenth century.

In this selection excerpted from his book *Forbidden Workers: Illegal Chinese Immigrants and American Labor*, Peter Kwong discusses the primarily poor, uneducated, and illegal Chinese immigrants brought into the country by "snakeheads." Snakeheads, or illegal people-smugglers, operate as part of a large and sophisticated international crime ring that smuggles workers into America. Once in the country, the immigrants are deeply in debt to the smugglers and find themselves held in virtual serfdom for years after entry. Kwong is the director of the Asian American Studies Program at Hunter College, City University of New York, and the author of *Chinatown, New York: Labor and Politics, 1930–1950* (1980) and *The New Chinatown* (1987, 1996).

Peter Kwong, *Forbidden Workers: Illegal Chinese Immigrants and American Labor.* New York: New Press, 1997. Copyright © 1998 by Peter Kwong. Reproduced by permission of The New Press. (800) 233-4830.

Chinese organized crime has developed human smuggling into a truly global business, shepherding some 100,000 people per year to a range of destinations including Taiwan, Japan, Germany, Canada, Australia, the United States, France, England, and the Netherlands. Stories of Chinese-run smuggling rings are ubiquitous. Japanese authorities found Chinese smugglers had been working with the *Yakuza*, the Japanese crime syndicate, to smuggle Chinese nationals into Japan through Tamara Island in the Tokara chain, south of Kyushu. The Chinese snakeheads charge as much as $25,000 to sneak job-seekers into Japan, and their *Yakuza* partners scout out quiet landing sites and use walkie-talkies to help guide the boat people safely ashore. . . .

The profits of the Chinese smuggling network are reported to be in the range of $3.1 billion U.S. per year. It is certainly an elaborate network. Indeed, Chinese transit operations seem to have penetrated every major airport and harbor around the world. According to a China Public Security Bureau estimate, at any time there are a half million Chinese nationals in smuggling waystations around the world—50,000 in Moscow, 15,000 in Ho Chi Minh City, 25,000 in Bangkok, 25,000 in Africa, 10,000 in Brazil, and thousands in other countries, including the Dominican Republic, Mexico, and Bulgaria.

Services and Fees

In the past, human smugglers simply provided assistance in border crossing, like the "coyotes" who charge at most a few hundred dollars for sneaking a client across the U.S.-Mexico border. Smuggling services are much more comprehensive today, and Chinese smugglers are among the most sophisticated. Their package includes passage out of China, a transit location or locations as the case requires, and transport to a final destination. Today's smugglers charge much higher fees for their services: anywhere from

$18,000 to $50,000 per customer.

The high fee has nothing to do with the actual cost of transportation, but it has transformed the relationship between the smuggler and the client from a simple one-shot deal—paid for up front, before the journey—into a complex financial arrangement that may last for many years. There is usually a complicated payment arrangement to be worked out after the client's arrival that may even require the smuggler to find them employment. The fee is paid either in installments or through loans from their relatives. The most important feature of this system is that even if the fees were paid by their relatives, they, too, have to borrow that large sum from others. The latter, in turn, expect fastidious repayment or face deadly consequences. In the end, the illegals would still have to work hard and fast to repay that amount promptly. The heavy debt burden gives the Chinese operations similarities to nineteenth-century coolie contract labor.

Smuggling into the United States

The most developed and best organized of all the Chinese smuggling routes leads to the United States. In testimony before Congress in 1994, then-director of the CIA James Woolsey Jr. claimed, according to his office's study, that some 100,000 Chinese are being smuggled into America each year. Many are sent first through Belize, Guatemala, the Dominican Republic, Mexico, or other countries in Central America and the Caribbean region. But, for most, the road starts in Fuzhou [a province in the People's Republic of China] and ends in New York.

Fuzhou has had a long history of illegal emigration, but the thrust of recent smuggling activities was sharpened by the United States' abrupt abandonment of its role in Vietnam. During the Sino-Vietnamese political crisis in 1978—after the American withdrawal from Saigon and the exodus of the Vietnamese boat people—almost one million Vietnamese of Chinese descent were resettled in China. Most of them were relocated in Guangxi Province [People's Republic of China] which borders Vietnam, but some refugees of Fuzhounese descent were repatriated back to Fuzhou's rural villages.

Unhappy with their relocation, many decided to pull up stakes and try again, hiring fishing vessels to carry them to Japan. In the early 1980s, dozens of fishing boats drifted into Japanese waters, and their passengers appealed for political asylum—rightly—as Vietnamese "boat people." Mixed among the legitimate refugees, however, were others who were less so.

Later, Taiwanese crime syndicates took over the Fuzhounese snakehead business, and the operation underwent various refinements. The basic strategy is to avoid detection en route and, when that is not possible, to look for new alternatives, including bribery. This means gaining the most up-to-date information about police plans in order to respond flexibly. Most of all, however, the syndicate's techniques exploit every weakness of national governments, including their limited reach beyond their borders, their lack of inter-government and intra-government coordination, legal loopholes, bureaucratic incompetence, and official corruption.

Chinese human smuggling is played like global baseball. The sprint to first base is the transfer of would-be illegal immigrants onto small fishing boats in Fuzhou and Wenzhou harbors for ferrying to international waters, where they will be picked up by Taiwanese seagoing vessels. Once fully loaded—shipping companies are paid per head—the ships sail southwest to Thailand for refueling before making a stab for second base. After crossing the Pacific, they land in the coastal areas of either Central America or Mexico, usually debarking aboard small fishing boats or pleasure craft. This sea route south of the United States avoids detection by American reconnaissance satellites, which monitor the U.S. coasts. Once on land, the smugglers use safe houses operated by Taiwanese nationals in La Paz, Bolivia, as the transit point.

Entry by Land

The dash to third base is the crossing of the U.S. border by land. If their ship docked in Central America, the smugglers travel through Mexico City, infiltrate the Texas border, and arrive in Atlanta, Georgia, or Houston, Texas. If it landed in Mexico's Baja California Peninsula, they cross the border into San Diego and rest in safe houses in largely Chinese American Monterey Park before flying on to home base, New York.

The route from Baja California is in fact an old Chinese trail. Today's elaborate border controls deterring Mexicans were originally established during the early decades of this century in response to illegal Chinese immigrants, who were banned from legal entry by the Chinese Exclusion Act of 1882. There is a small fishing village, Punta China, in Baja California, so named for being the favorite landing spot for Chinese ships carrying illegals.

There are dozens of variations on this sea/land route. Xiao Lin, the butcher's son, and several others from the [ship] *Golden Venture*[1] took a different road, to Thailand. They were transported by train to Kunming in Yunan Province, southwest of China near the Burmese border, where they transferred to a bus that took them to the border town of Pu-erh. From there they rode on horseback through thick Burmese jungles. It took them two to three weeks of strenuous journeying to reach Thailand and eventually Bangkok. Along the way they rested at Chinese-

1. The *Golden Venture* was an immigrant-smuggling ship whose passengers had a particularly harrowing voyage to America in 1993; many of the refugees were deported back to China.

operated guest houses as they passed through the notorious "Golden Triangle" on the Burma-China-Thailand borders, the world's most important heroin production center. They traveled, in fact, along the principal heroin trafficking route to Bangkok. Intelligence reports suggest that the human smugglers have close contacts with the heroin traffickers, who are controlled by the overseas Chaozhounese syndicate (Chaozhou is in the northeastern coastal region of Guangdong Province).

Some illegals, who came to the United States by land through Mexico aboard chartered private planes, report seeing other private planes on the illegal Mexican landing strip that were used by drug traffickers. So, it appears, Chinese snakeheads have connections with the cocaine cartels in South America as well.

Entry by Air

The most comfortable and the fastest route to America is, of course, by air. It requires, however, that the smuggled individuals have legal visas for transit countries. For 300 yuan ($45 U.S.), one can get an "official invitation" from a Russian company enabling Chinese citizens to obtain Russian entry visas. Once in Moscow, the U.S.-bound illegals begin to maneuver, trying to arrange visas to enter other transit countries. This may take weeks, and the snakeheads have already set up Moscow coordination centers, complete with hostels established just for Chinese illegals. The trick is to get to a transit country whose airport security is so lax or, more likely, so corrupt that it would let Chinese with questionable identification papers board a U.S.-bound plane. The moment an illegal is on a plane headed for the United States, he is virtually home free, for even if his fake documents are detected, he can always request political asylum and stay. . . .

A surer way to enter the United States painlessly is to

obtain a second set of documents—either a stolen or a fake Taiwanese, Indonesian, or Argentinean passport with a "valid" tourist visa for entry to the United States. Several Central American countries' consulate employees stationed in Hong Kong working with smuggling rings provide future aliens with travel papers without requesting identification. Another way to avoid airline detection altogether is to fly to Cuba, the Dominican Republic, or the Bahamas, then board a chartered fishing boat to Puerto Rico or the U.S. Virgin Island of St. John. Once there, New York is within reach via a domestic flight.

Entry by Sea

With the possibility of putting five or six clients on a flight and so many scheduled commercial flights to choose from, air transport can be surprisingly efficient. Yet the cost per head is higher and it is very chancy. Smuggling by sea is certainly cheaper and is used extensively. Between 1991 and 1993, thirty-two ships with a total of as many as 5,300 Chinese aboard were found by various immigration authorities in the waters off Japan, Taiwan, Singapore, Guatemala, El Salvador, Australia, Haiti, and the United States. Of course, many more went undetected. . . .

The majority of the ships used for human smuggling have been of Taiwanese origin. Although Taiwan has a large ocean-going fishing fleet, the ships employed for this purpose are usually on their last legs, crudely converted for their new purpose. Many are unseaworthy. Sometimes they end up drifting for days awaiting repairs, and as a last resort some have even had to send out distress signals. In order to save money, none of the standard safety features or sanitation facilities required for transporting large numbers of people are available on board. The snakeheads even skimp on fuel and provisions. The sea journey, always slow, is now even longer as the ships evade the Navy and moor offshore in international waters, waiting for local snakeheads to arrange for chartered local craft to pick up the passengers.

Snakeheads can be very cruel at sea. When the Coast Guard boarded the disguised trawler *Jung Sheng No. 8* off Hawaii in June 1996, they found 120 men packed into a tight, twenty-by-thirty-foot camouflaged compartment that had been nailed shut without ventilation. The men were naked and had been held between decks for several weeks without showers; they were caged in their own waste, and ate in a mass-feeding area where bowls were nailed to the table. Eight women were held in the converted stateroom on the main deck. Many aliens on the ship suffered from skin and urinary tract infections due to dehydration and unsanitary conditions. One of the Coast Guard officers who boarded the ship recalled: "When we pulled the hatch on the hold, we were overwhelmed with the rush of hot steamy air that smelled of urine and fecal matter"; and that it "just never went away."

The smugglers had recruited enforcers to terrorize the illegals during the voyage. They would hold them down while others beat them, force them to drink sea water, or force them to perform sexual acts. The enforcers tried to extort anything valuable from the passengers to drive them even further into debt. They even came up with the idea of making their captives sign IOUs for phony gambling debts in their own blood, cutting their fingers and pressing their bloody fingerprints onto receipts.

The barbaric conditions—hardly atypical—on *Jung Sheng No. 8* stunned the Coast Guard boarding party. They were scarcely better than those suffered by the slaves brought from Africa in the eighteenth and nineteenth centuries.

Inhumane Conditions

A special feature of Chinese smuggling operations is the extensive involvement of smugglers with the clients after they arrive in the United States. Usually the snakeheads hold the illegal immigrants in safe houses until all their debts are paid. The payment schedule is clearly stipulated in a standard contract, which states that the would-be immigrants had to deliver a down payment before they started the journey to cover the cost of "registration" and their transportation, none of which is refundable. The remainder is to be paid after they arrive in New York.

In the early stages of the human smuggling industry, some snakeheads extended credit, allowing their clients to pay the debt off in monthly installments. However, as the smuggling business grew, keeping track of credit allowances became a nuisance. Also, a lengthy involvement with a freely roaming client made brushes with law enforcement more likely. These days, smugglers insist on the full final payment before releasing the illegals. They prefer to shift the responsibility of keeping track of the debt payments to other enforcement parties, be they relatives, local gangs, local loan sharks, or village associations. Indeed, they often insist that the final payment be completed in China, in order to avoid the need to launder their money in the United States and thus risk detection by the authorities. This means that the relatives of the smuggled aliens have to transfer their funds back to China through illegitimate money-laundering services in Chinatown. An illegal immigrant held in New York is released only after a phone call from the snaketail in China confirms the completion of the transaction.

The worst abuses of illegal immigrants occur in New York safe houses while they wait for their relatives to come up with the final payment. To encourage the relatives to raise the funds by borrowing from various sources more quickly, the smuggling networks contract with non-Fuzhounese youth gangs—sometimes American-born Chinese, other times Vietnamese—as enforcers. Members of the infamous Vietnamese Born to Kill gang, known for their mindlessly indiscriminate violence, were once hired for such services. The enforcers begin to abuse the illegals as soon as they arrive at the safe houses, at times forcing them to talk to their relatives on the phone while undergoing torture.

The police claim that there are some 300 safe houses holding newcomers in New York City. They are usually located in basement cellars, and all illegals have to spend some time in one before being released. The immigrants are obliged to eat, sleep, and urinate in the same place as more than a dozen inmates, all of whom are confined to one room. They are starved, deprived of fresh air and sunlight, and beaten regularly. At times they are ordered to inflict pain on each other. Many are shackled and handcuffed to metal bed frames. Males are told that they could be killed; the females are threatened with work in a whorehouse.

Some men have in fact been killed to set an example to others, and girls have in fact been forced to work in massage parlors for years without pay; others end up locked in during the day and forced to work at gambling joints at night. One thing the smugglers always make sure of is that their victims do not dare to inform the authorities or testify against them in court—not even to talk about their experience with other illegals. They are never allowed to forget that the smugglers control the whole community. They should see no evil, hear no evil, and mind their own business after their release.

CHAPTER 4

Portraits of Chinese Americans

COMING TO AMERICA

Musician Yo-Yo Ma

David Blum

Yo-Yo Ma, the son of Chinese parents who emigrated from China to France, was born in Paris in 1955. When he was seven, the family immigrated to the United States and settled in New York. By that time, it was already apparent that Ma was a musical prodigy. Yet Ma's youth and early adulthood was a time of intense turmoil. He often felt caught between the expectations of his traditional Chinese parents and the lure of the American culture around him. Ma also struggled to resolve the tension between his desire to achieve expertise and discipline in his music while at the same time developing his musical creativity and originality. In this excerpt from his book *Quintet*, David Blum encourages Ma to tell in his own words how he resolved this tension. Today Yo-Yo Ma is considered the foremost cellist in the world. Blum, who died in 1998, was a respected conductor and the author of several books on musicians, including *Casals and the Art of Interpretation.*

According to ancient Chinese custom, every family keeps a book in which the names for many generations ahead are planned. All family members from a particular generation will share a single written character. *Yo*, which in Chinese means "friendship," is the generational character for Ma and his sister, Yeou-Cheng. "With me they seem to have got lazy and been unable to think of anything else, so they added another Yo," [Yo-Yo Ma] said one day as we talked in Zurich. "In China, as in Hungary, a person is addressed by the last name first; I would be called Ma Yo-Yo. (Inci-

David Blum, *Quintet: Five Journeys Toward Musical Fulfillment.* Ithaca, NY: Cornell University Press, 1988. Copyright © 1988 by David Blum. Reproduced by permission of the publisher.

dentally, *Ma* means 'horse.') It means something philosophically, doesn't it, when you state your family name as your primary identity? Throughout the Orient, the family is the basic unit, and the society as a whole is a larger family. The Japanese have a word, *amae*, which is the feeling a baby gets when it's being breast-fed—the feeling of being totally loved, enveloped, and nurtured. This is how the individual feels in Oriental society. The Orient is based less on dialogue than on monologue. In the Confucian hierarchy, you're always placing somebody above or below you. The role of every family member is defined. For instance, my sister loves her little brother, and will do everything for me. She does this of her own free will, but it's also culturally expected. If the youngster goes significantly against the system he brings shame on the family." Ma's parents adhered to these traditions.

Ma's Parents

Ma's father, Hiao-Tsiun Ma, was born into a landowning family in Ningbo, a city south of Shanghai. He decided to devote his life to music, learned to play the violin, and eventually became a professor at Nanjing University. Education was highly prized in Chinese society; the small scholar-gentry class was accorded the greatest respect. But after the emergence of Sun Yat-sen, in 1911, China entered into a prolonged period of cultural and political instability, and the structure of life changed rapidly; conditions were often chaotic. Educated Chinese increasingly gravitated to the West. In 1936, Hiao-Tsiun left for Paris to further his musical studies. Ma's mother, Marina, was born in Hong Kong. ("The southerners are generally warm and temperamental," Ma says.) Gifted with a beautiful voice, she first met Hiao-Tsiun at Nanjing, as a student in his music-theory class. In 1949, she, too, moved to Paris. There they were married, and there Yo-Yo was born, on

October 7, 1955, four years after the birth of his sister.

"My father was a born pedagogue," Ma told me. "He wanted not only to advance himself through learning but to share that learning. He wanted to teach everybody; it was a way of life. He taught languages and music to his brother and his two sisters, and even claimed that he had taught a dog how to sing." Hiao-Tsiun tutored his children in French history, Chinese history, mythology, and calligraphy. Yeou-Cheng studied the violin with Arthur Grumiaux, and Yo-Yo took up the piano and the cello. His cello teacher, Michelle Lepinte, was astonished when the four-year-old, under his father's guidance began to play a Bach suite. Hiao-Tsiun had developed a method of teaching young children how to concentrate intensively. No more than a short assignment was given daily, but this was to be thoroughly assimilated. He proceeded systematically and patiently. Each day, Yo-Yo was expected to memorize two measures of Bach; the following day, two more measures. He learned to recognize patterns—their similarities and their differences—and soon developed a feeling for musical structure. By the time he was five, he had learned three Bach suites. The same technique was applied to a host of études. "I found this method ideal, because I didn't like to work hard," Ma recalled. "When problems in cello technique arose, my father would apply the principle '*Coupez la difficulté en quatre*' [cut the problem into fourths]. This helped me to avoid the kind of strain young cellists often experience. When a problem is complex, you become tense, but when you break it down into basic components you can approach each element without stress. Then, when you put it all together, you do something that seems externally complex, but you don't feel it that way. You know it from several different angles."

Chinese calligraphy was taught by the same method. Hiao-Tsiun prepared several hundred cards, each one marked with a character and an explanation of it in French. Yo-Yo was required to learn two characters a day, and to keep a diary in Chinese. He says that he still knows French because his father gave him a paragraph to memorize every morning before going to school. These French studies included formal écriture. "If you've noticed my penmanship, you'll see how I've since rebelled," he said. "However, my father's pedagogical techniques have proved invaluable. When I was twelve, Leonard Rose"—with whom Ma studied at the Juilliard School—"assigned me the Dvořák Concerto. I was unbelievably excited. When I got home, my father said, 'Let's get down to work.' At the end of six hours, I had memorized the whole first movement. Last year, I gave myself ten days to learn two major works, by Barber and Britten, both for cello and orchestra. I had looked at the scores but had never played them on the cello. It was irresponsible of me. They were a horrible ten days—but I succeeded."

Immigration to America

Ma's musical studies progressed so rapidly that he was able at the age of five to give a concert at the University of Paris, playing both the cello and the piano. But his life was soon to change radically. In 1962, Hiao-Tsiun received news that his brother, who had recently emigrated to America, was discouraged and was thinking of returning to China. Gathering up his life savings, Hiao-Tsiun hurried his family to New York and managed to persuade his brother to stay on. Hiao-Tsiun had planned to visit for six months; he remained for sixteen years. Once he was established in the New World, he formed the Children's Orchestra of New York, and a generation of youngsters benefitted from his exceptional gifts as a teacher. Yo-Yo began lessons with Janos Scholz, the distinguished cellist, who is also noted for his collection of Italian Master drawings.

Scholz remembers Ma as "the most natural and eager boy you could imagine," and says, "He was adored by my whole family. We went through a mountain of repertoire in two years. He learned with lightning speed. He was everything one could wish for as a student, and the last I ever took."

Ma is loath to admit that as a child he actually enjoyed playing the cello. He remembers chiefly the rigors of memorization, the absorption of endless bits and pieces of information. Despite all, he performed with a freshness and an enthusiasm that captivated his listeners. Isaac Stern is a witness. "I first heard Yo-Yo play in Paris when he was five or six years old," he says. "The cello was literally larger than he was. I could sense then, as has now been confirmed, that he has one of the most extraordinary talents of this generation. I was so taken by him that when he was nine I arranged for him to study with Leonard Rose. Lenny told me that, unlike any other student he could remember, Yo-Yo would come to every lesson perfectly prepared. It's not just that he had practiced. He played every piece from memory and had obviously worked constantly on everything he had been assigned. He bloomed under Lenny.". . .

Caught Between Two Cultures

If the move to America opened new horizons for the Ma family, it posed problems as well. "America was my father's third culture, and it was hard for him to adjust," Ma said. "One of the duties of an Oriental child is unquestioning obedience to the parents; this is supposed to continue throughout one's life. It goes beyond obedience; the parents identify completely with the child. When I got into trouble, it was not considered my fault; it was somebody else's fault. I couldn't have deliberately done anything wrong, because I was, after all, an extension of my parents. As soon as we moved to America I had to deal with two contradictory worlds. At home, I was to submerge my identity. You can't talk back to your parents—period. At school, I was expected to answer back, to reveal my individuality. At home, we spoke only Chinese; we were taken to Chinese movies to remind us of our traditional values. But I was also American, growing up with American values. I became aware that if I was to be a cellist playing concertos I would have to have ideas of my own; that's one of the great things about being a musician. My conflict was apparent to Pablo Casals, to whom I was presented when I was seven. I don't remember what he said about my cello playing, but he did suggest that I should be given more time to go out and play in the street.

"My home life was totally structured. Because I couldn't rebel there, I did so at school. In the fifth grade, I began to cut classes, and I continued doing so through high school. I spent a lot of time wandering through the streets, mainly because I just wanted to be alone." Eventually, in 1968, Ma entered the Professional Children's School, in New York, but he missed so many classes that his teachers concluded that he was bored and would be better off in an accelerated program. That program enabled him to graduate from high school when he was fifteen. He spent the following summer at Ivan Galamian's camp for string players, at Meadowmount, in the Adirondacks. It was his first experience on his own, away from home.

"Suddenly, I was free," Ma told me. "I had always kept my emotions bottled up, but at Meadowmount I just ran wild, as if I'd been let out of a ghetto. The whole structure of discipline collapsed. I exploded into bad taste at every level. Mr. Galamian was concerned that the boys and girls maintain a certain decorum. He would say, 'They shouldn't go into the bushes together.' I took some white paint and decorated the stone walls with graffiti on the subject. When Galamian found out, he was horrified. I knew I had gone too far, and spent a whole day washing the walls. I would leave my cello outside, not worrying if it might rain, and run off to play Ping-Pong. That summer, I played the Schubert Arpeggione Sonata and the Franck Sonata with uninhibited freedom—just letting go, in a way that had never happened before.". . .

"This Guy Is Trouble"

Yeou-Cheng was now at Radcliffe; Yo-Yo had been tempted to apply to Harvard, but after his experience at Meadowmount his instinct told him that he was too young to take that step. He entered Columbia University, meanwhile continuing his lessons with Leonard Rose, at Juilliard. It seemed an ideal way to combine music with academics, but difficulties arose. "I was still living at home and trying to do a lot of things," Ma said. "I still felt as if I were going to high school." He eventually dropped out of Columbia, without telling his parents.

Ma then spent his days hanging about at Juilliard, trying to act older than he was. He acquired a fake I.D. card so that he could drink. During breaks in orchestra rehearsals, he would run to the liquor store and buy a bottle of Scotch to hand around when playing resumed. "One day, I passed out in a practice room, having thrown up all over the place. They thought I had O.D.'d on drugs. So they carted me off by ambulance to Roosevelt Hospital, where they recognized that I was suffering from the effects of alcohol. As I was a minor, my parents were sent for. A moment of deep shame in the Ma household. My father thought that if his son had become an alcoholic he himself should set an example through self-denial. He had always reserved for himself one special treat: a glass of wine before dinner. So he gave up this glass for four years. The other repercussions were enormous. I was called into the dean's office. Leonard Rose was informed, and, concerned that I was under too much pressure, arranged for me to see a psychiatrist. The news of my drinking spread to friends in France. All I was trying to do was to be accepted as one of the guys, and not be considered a freak. But for the next five years everywhere I went people would look at me and think, This guy is trouble. When I'd arrive late at a rehearsal, or entirely forget to come, everybody thought the worst." Even today, Ma is slightly abashed to recall his teen-age misconduct. From the American point of view, such episodes were typical adolescent behavior; from the Chinese point of view, they were grave transgressions.

"In college, even until I was in my twenties, I fought against the whole principle of discipline," Ma went on. "I was meshuga [Yiddish for 'crazy'] I didn't know when to go to sleep or when to do my laundry. I learned to drive in three days, and had a couple of car crashes that people knew about and a couple that no one ever found out about."

College Life

Ma was nearly seventeen and had reached a crossroads: Should he pursue a full-time musical career or go to Harvard? Isaac Stern recalls, "During those growing years—whatever growing pains there were—Yo-Yo made a decision rather remarkable for a talented young man of his age, and that was to try to get an education. He could have devoted all his time to preparing pieces for concerts and competitions, but he took the unusual step of deciding to become a person. He may have been influenced by his Chinese background, with its tremendous respect for the value of learning. In any event, he went through Harvard, keeping his music up while taking a full course of studies. Those two things don't ordinarily go together." In four years at Harvard, in addition to studying music, he took courses in the rise and fall of civilizations, Chinese and Japanese history, anthropology, French civilization, fine arts, modern Chinese literature, German literature, Dostoyevski, astronomy, math, sociology, and natural sciences. When I asked how he had found time to combine such studies with his career as a cellist, he said, "I was able to manage because I was unbelievably lazy in everything. I had very low standards—I didn't feel compelled to get high grades, or to practice many hours every day. I worked in spurts. If I could no longer put off writing a paper, I studied into the night. And when I had a concert to give and didn't want to make an absolute fool of myself I'd put in a few more hours of practice. Once, when I hadn't listened to the works assigned for a music exam, I jimmied the lock of the music library and heard a semester's worth of music in one night. In my freshman year, I overslept and missed an exam and was put on probation. That was a bad moment. But my generally undisciplined approach to life offers me the possibility of doing many things. I didn't apply myself sufficiently in high school to learn how to do research or how to write papers. Yet I was curious about things. I wanted to try to tie together the various threads of my life—my Chinese upbringing, the atmosphere of Paris, my totally different experience in America. Studying history was a way of putting these diverse cultures in perspective, and studying anthropology—the !Kung people of the Kalahari desert, the Yanomamö of Venezuela—helped me to understand better the tremendous variety of values in all of humanity.". . .

Learning How to Learn

During his Harvard years, Ma made his London début, performing the Elgar Concerto with the Royal Philharmonic Orchestra, conducted by Yehudi Menuhin. The concerts started accumulating, and Ma felt that it would be possible for him to make a living as a musician. In fact, he was so inundated with concerts that his academic work suffered. "I even thought of leaving school, but my father insisted that I stay, and limit my concerts to one a month," he said. "In retrospect, I'm happy I followed his advice." Isaac Stern says of Ma's experience at Harvard, "He learned musical analysis and a good deal about life in general. But, above all, he learned how to learn—something that may be the most important thing a young person can do in any profession. He learned how to apply himself in the best possible way to everything he needed for his artistic development."

Athlete Michelle Kwan

Michelle Kwan, as told to Laura James

Michelle Kwan, one of the world's greatest figure skaters, is a five-time world champion, seven-time U.S. national champion, and a two-time Olympic medalist. In this selection from her autobiography, *Heart of a Champion*, Kwan recounts the story of her parents' meeting, marriage, and emigration from Hong Kong to America. Kwan explains that she is close to her family, often speaks Chinese at home, and has enjoyed visiting her relatives in China. Kwan sees parallels between her hard work and dedication on the ice and the hard work and dedication her parents showed when they immigrated to America.

My parents, Danny and Estella, were born in China. My mother was born in Hong Kong where she had a happy childhood and a big, loving family. She was an excellent student, and she loved music and ballet. When she was a teenager she was like I am now in lots of ways. That's probably why we get along so well!

She worked hard but also liked to have fun. And, like me, she never did anything without first thinking through all the consequences very carefully. It takes us both a long time to make decisions, even little ones.

Michelle's Father

My father was born in a little village near the Chinese city of Canton (now called Guang-zhou). From what I've heard, life in China has changed and improved a lot since he was a kid. But back in the days of his childhood, life could be hard. . . .

My dad tells about how he would get up at four o'clock in the morning to be the first in line to buy a small portion of meat. He didn't go to school or even meet his father until he was eight years old. But he learned a lot of lessons about life that school never could have taught him.

By the time my father was eight, my grandfather had moved to Hong Kong. Once he was settled, he sent for his family. My father started attending the school where my mother was also a student. Their families were friends, so they got to know each other.

Dad says he always had a little crush on Mom, but it was a long time before they fell in love. Anyway, I don't think they had much in common in those days: My mother was one of the best students, and my father, who had a lot of catching up to do, was near the bottom of the class.

My dad started working when he was thirteen years old. Even then he was ambitious, with big dreams for the future. He was a messenger for a few years, and later got a job working for the telephone company. He first came to America in 1971, when he was twenty-two, to attend a family wedding in California. He saw a chance to make the kind of life he'd always dreamed of, and he decided to stay.

He started out working in a restaurant, where he learned to cook. Then he also took a job with the telephone company in Los Angeles. Pretty soon, he and a partner opened up their own restaurant, the Golden Pheasant, in Torrance, which is just south of L.A. He worked very hard. He wanted to succeed.

Michelle's Mother

Meanwhile, my mother was in Hong Kong, working as a nurse in a hospital. She loved taking care of people, but it was hard for her to watch them suffer. She needed a change, and (after thinking it over a lot) she made a big one—she became a television news anchorwoman!

That's what she was doing the next time she saw my father, when he came home to Hong Kong for their school reunion. And that's when they fell in love.

Soon they got married and moved back to the United States together. My mother, my father, and both of his parents lived in Torrance, and everybody helped out at the Golden Pheasant. Ron was born first, and then Karen came two years later.

My parents felt like they had a full house. "That's enough!" they said. "No more kids for now." They didn't want to see any of their kids suffering because there wasn't enough to go around.

Michelle's Birth

But surprise! On July 7, 1980, I came into the world. My father named me Michelle, after his favorite song by his favorite band, the Beatles. It's a song about a boy who loves a girl, a beautiful girl with a beautiful name—Michelle.

We speak a mixture of Chinese and English at home. My father tells lots of stories about the old life in China. I always—even when I skate—wear a necklace that my grandmother gave me. It has a little Chinese dragon on it and a symbol that means good luck. Karen, Ron, and I are very close to our grandparents. Even though they don't speak much English, we understand one another.

I've been to China twice—once to skate, not long ago. The first time I was there was when I was very little and my mother took us to Hong Kong to meet her side of the family. I was too young then to remember much about that trip now, but Mom always says she's so glad she took us. Just a little while after we were there, her mother—my grandmother—died. It was so nice that she'd seen us and hugged us first.

But life in China still seems so far away from my life, and so different. Where did my competitive spirit come from? How did my parents end up with a daughter like me, who is so completely into one sport?

Actually, I can see similarities between what I do and what my parents did in coming to America. They wanted to start a family in a place where they could work hard and keep their kids happy and healthy. America was a faraway dream to them, but they believed in it and made it come true.

When I was little, my dream of becoming a world-class skater was far away, too. But I learned from my parents that if you work hard enough, your dream just might come true.

Scientist and Physician David Ho

David Ho, in an interview with the Academy of Achievement

When he was twelve, David Ho immigrated with his family to California from Taiwan, an island off the coast of China that was traditionally controlled and inhabited by the Chinese. In this interview for the Academy of Achievement, an interactive Web-based museum featuring individuals who have made significant contributions to their fields, Ho describes his childhood and his early college career. Although he liked physics and mathematics, Ho quickly became interested in molecular biology and eventually attended medical school. While working as chief resident in internal medicine at the University of California, Los Angeles, he began to see the earliest victims of the AIDS epidemic.

Ho became deeply interested in AIDS and started researching the disease. His contribution has been twofold. First, he discovered that the human immunodeficiency virus, which causes AIDS, is most active immediately after infection. That means the infected person must be treated immediately after a positive test. Second, he and a team of researchers developed a "cocktail" of drugs, including protease inhibitors, which saved millions of people from dying of AIDS. Indeed, the number of deaths from AIDS dropped by two-thirds in the two years after the introduction of Ho's drug cocktail. Ho was named *Time* Man of the Year in 1996, and he is now director of the

Academy of Achievement, "Interview with David Ho," www.achievement.org, May 23, 1998. Copyright © 1998 by the Academy of Achievement. All rights reserved. Reproduced by permission.

Aaron Diamond AIDS Research Center in New York City, where he is working on a vaccine for AIDS.

Academy of Achievement: Dr. Ho, you were born in Taiwan. Perhaps you could tell us a little about your childhood. What was life like in your home town?

David Ho: Tai Chung at that time was a pretty small city. We lived at the edge of the city, sort of bordering on the rice fields. I remember that my father had left Taiwan to come to the United States to pursue graduate studies in engineering, and so my brother and I were left in my mother's care, and so in essence grew up in Taiwan without my father being present. But he was pursuing something that we all viewed as very important, very scholarly type of work.

In Taiwan you had to take these entrance examinations for junior high school, and everybody wanted to go to the best school. So as little kids we were already subjected to a fair amount of pressure. I remember having to study a lot. Because of what my father did, there was a great deal of emphasis on scholarly endeavors. . . .

Do you remember how you felt when he was ready to have you come [to America]?

Excitement, at the same time some level of concern. This is something that we had looked forward to for a long time, so it was great to know it was finally upon us. I was only 12 years old at the time, but I realized it was going to be dramatically different for me, my mother and my brother. We were going to a country that is completely different from Taiwan culturally, linguistically, and in many other aspects as well. There was this anxiety that brewed and brewed, and it certainly came true when we landed. It's an entirely different culture, and culture shock is a good description of the initial phase. I had done fairly well in school in Taiwan. I came here and all of a sudden I couldn't communicate. It was a devastating period.

School was nearly impossible even though I went every day, not being able to comprehend what the teacher and the classmates are saying, and not being able to express any thoughts, because at that stage we hadn't even learned the ABC's. And so, it was very, very difficult for a period of about three months.

Is it true that your father didn't want you to learn English until you got to America?

He wanted to be sure that we learned English appropriately. Of course, the English taught in Taiwan would be accented, but it might also be not completely correct, and he didn't see much point to it. One would be learning extremely slowly and it might make a difference of a week or two, but I think in the end he was correct. We were immersed in this new world, and you had to pick it up. As a child, one is flexible enough to do that quickly. It went fast, and by the end of the first six months or so, both my brother and I were picking up enough to get along in school.

Learning English

Did the school system make any extra effort to teach you English?

We had extra English classes to attend in addition to some of the regular classes, but there was no bilingual program at the time.

Where did you live when you first came to America? What was it like?

This was in 1965 in Los Angeles. Well, for a few months. When I first came, I hadn't finished elementary school education, and my father was just . . . starting a new job and finishing his studies at USC [University of Southern California]. So we lived near USC in what is today a predominantly black neighborhood. Whether it was white or black, it was all culture shock to me. We were there for a few months, and then moved nearer to the Los Feliz neighborhood some months later. I went to King Junior High and Marshall High School near Los Feliz.

When you first arrived in Los Angeles and couldn't speak English, the kids probably were not very sympathetic. How did they treat you?

I encountered an array of receptions from the kids. As you might expect, some kids are cruel, and if you can't say anything, they make fun of you. They call you stupid or other names. But there are also a lot of kids who are quite reasonable, who try to help. I certainly remember a lot of them. Sure, when other kids are being cruel, it's very, very tough, and then you have nothing to come back with simply because you can't express yourself.

But I must emphasize that was only a short period of time.

What was your ambition growing up?

I was always interested in pursuing science, not because of any particular role model, but because I was curious. I wanted to learn about things, ask questions. As I came to the U.S., I naturally gravitated in that direction, not so much in medical science at first, but in physics and related topics. I went to Cal Tech [California Institute of Technology] to study physics, although during the later years I developed an interest in the new molecular biology, and that was what led me . . . into medical research.

Didn't you also spend some time at MIT [Massachusetts Institute of Technology]?

As an undergraduate I spent one year at MIT and three years at Cal Tech. I got into both schools, and I had a great deal of ambivalence about where to go. People were kind enough to allow me to set up a hybrid program and I got to experience both institutions. Obviously, I had to devote more time at one than the other, and I was attracted to Cal

Tech because of figures like Richard Feynman and Murray Gell-Mann, giants of physics.

Favorite Books, Favorite Studies

[What] books were extremely important to you when you were growing up?

I was reading a fair amount of science fiction as well as science written for the general public. Although some of it was certainly way over my head, I still remember reading books by Isaac Asimov, science fiction stories, and also books by physicists, talking about things that normal people can't readily conceive of, like anti-matter. It was just interesting to try to think in that way, even though I wasn't understanding everything.

I was curious about all these things I couldn't understand and I tried to learn more by reading more. Gradually a little bit would sink in. Looking back, I must admit my understanding was quite sketchy, but it was that kind of curiosity that drove me into science. I remember going to the library and trying to look at the Feynman lectures in physics. That's very fundamental physics, nothing too fancy, but presented in his unusual style. I hadn't taken all the requisite courses before reading it, I was just very interested by it.

How did your parents respond to your choice of physics and then molecular biology?

My parents never tried to influence my decisions. They pretty much left it up to me. I wasn't a troubled child. I was doing well in school, so they said to do what you like, which is the same attitude I now have with my own kids: "Just do what you like. You have to pursue what you're interested in. Just do it well, whatever you pick."

Why did you switch from physics to molecular biology?

In high school my biology was just trying to remember the names of various animal species, plant species, and it was not all that exciting. But in my sophomore and junior year of college, I realized that there was a lot of fascinating new biology coming along. The era of molecular biology using recombinant DNA techniques was also just emerging, and that was fascinating. That hit me the same way some of the questions in the physical sciences did.

I got very interested and could appreciate the fact that medical research based on the new biology could have immediate applications if one were to apply those techniques to specific illnesses. I was most interested in things like particle physics and astrophysics, but those things are much less tangible day to day. In trying to talk to your friends and relatives, it's very hard to convey what you're actually doing and why you're doing it. Through a long and slow period I finally decided that I was going to continue to pursue science in the form of medical research. I had already taken enough biology and other courses to meet the requirements for medical school, so I made the transition. I wanted to pursue science, because it's what I loved to do. But the fact that by pursuing medical science you could also indirectly help people, made it even more a reason for doing that. . . .

How did medical school change you? Did it change your personality or your outlook?

Medical school per se did not change my personality. It was difficult for me to adjust at the beginning. At Cal Tech . . . we had take-home exams. They were very difficult problems. You could open any book you want, you just have to solve problems. In medical school you had to memorize everything. That transition initially was difficult. In terms of personality, the biggest event in my life was coming to the States from Taiwan. From being a fairly outgoing child I retreated and became rather reserved for a number of years. It took the late high school years, college years and medical school years, to reemerge, having gained greater confidence.

Was there a teacher along the way who was especially important to you?

There were teachers who put in a lot of effort to make sure I learned English. There were teachers in junior high school who appreciated the fact that even though my English wasn't up to par, I was particularly good in certain classes, and put me in with the more advanced students despite the language handicap. In high school, there were teachers who recognized my particular interest in chemistry and physics, and allowed me to do more than the usual students. . . .

Encountering AIDS

You were quite young when you first encountered AIDS, but no one knew what AIDS was. Where were you when you first encountered it?

I finished medical school at Harvard and went to train in internal medicine at UCLA. I was getting ready to pursue research on viruses. Then I was asked to stay on as a chief resident for an extra year. As a chief resident, you see a lot of patients. You hear about all the patients that are admitted. It was during that period that I heard from the interns and residents that the night before a man had come into the hospital with severe pneumonia. He couldn't breathe, and had to be put in the ICU [intensive care unit]. Pneumonia had wiped out both lungs, but at the same time he also had gastrointestinal problems and seizures, as if there was something else in the brain. This man died very quickly. His pneumonia was due to a parasite called pneumocystis carinae that only occurred in patients who were getting chemotherapy. There was another parasite in the brain, and a virus in the gastrointestinal tract, and this man some weeks before had been "perfectly healthy." We couldn't explain the illness.

We knew what the complications were, but we couldn't

explain the illness. We saw another one a few weeks later, and then another one, and the common link was that these were all young gay men. Upon taking a closer history, we found that they were gay men with lots of sexual contacts. They didn't have exactly the same set of complications, but the conclusion was that something was wiping out their immune system, allowing them to be sick with all of these other things. We were very concerned that something was being transmitted which is capable of destroying the immune system. Without thinking too much, we already believed that this had to be something new, something that wasn't in the textbooks, and in fact that turned out to be the case. I began with an interest in this medical curiosity, never realizing that this was going to be a big health problem for the public.

But the scientific aspect was extremely interesting in that here we were looking at something that was transmissible, capable of destroying the immune system. That was new, and one way or another the science behind that would shed light on bugs and on the immune system. So, I was gung ho from day one of the epidemic. . . .

What were your first important discoveries about HIV and AIDS?

I saw the first patient in 1981. By '82 I had moved to Boston to pursue research on viruses, and I continued to look for the cause. The cause was initially identified by scientists at the Pasteur Institute, and then confirmed by scientists at the NIH [National Institutes of Health]. I had a more substantial role beginning in 1984 when my colleagues and I showed that the virus is not just in people who are sick, but in people who are very healthy who belong in the same risk group. We were the first to show that there is a carrier state that can last for a long period of time.

You can be HIV positive, feel well, but still be carrying lots of virus?

That's exactly right. Moving on, we showed that the

virus, in addition to attacking the immune system, actually could attack the central nervous system. Particularly for late stage patients, there's a great deal of involvement of the brain, causing dementia in some severe cases. We also found an illness, associated with the initial phase of infection, that looked like flu. It lasted for several weeks then disappeared. During that phase, the patient has an enormous amount of virus before the immune system begins to kick in to keep it in check. My research has focused on trying to understand how the replication of the virus results in the depletion of the immune system. There had been an old dogma in the field that HIV comes in, and after this acute phase that looks like flu, there's a prolonged dormancy.

The virus wasn't doing much and the person is pretty well. And we know that, because we now know that period could be about ten years. And somehow, we realized that during this period the person's immune system is gradually dwindling, and I didn't necessarily like the notion that—we knew the patient is well—but I didn't necessarily like the notion that the virus is dormant. And for a long period of time, my research effort [was] to measure the virus, to quantify the virus. And I would say that's a decade long effort, having been one of the first to measure how much virus there is, and then very gradually demonstrating that the old notion is incorrect.

In fact, the virus comes in and grows and churns out lots of virus each day. It's destroying lots of immune cells each day, and the body has to pump out more of those cells to keep up. So we ultimately proved the old notion was incorrect. We're dealing with a highly dynamic virus and a highly dynamic process of replacing the lost cells. . . .

Success with Protease Inhibitors

Did you ever feel disheartened or want to quit and do something easier than this?

I felt disheartened and beaten for a long time. Even though the science was coming out positively, we weren't making much progress for the patients. So as scientists we could sit and celebrate each successful experiment, but we made very little difference to the lives of patients with HIV infection, and that was very disheartening.

And seeing lots of patients go over that decade and almost a decade and a half is quite devastating, but I never said, "This is too disheartening. I'm going to quit." We were learning so much about the virus, one optimistically could expect some progress to come along. And in fact, it did come along in 1994 when the protease inhibitors first went into human testing.

We had worked on such inhibitors in the laboratory in the late '80s and early '90s. No one paid any attention, and it was only through the clinical application and the results that the recognition came. We now had a powerful tool to fight HIV, and people were finding out that combining the older drugs was also powerful. We were strategically placed in 1994 to combine the protease inhibitors with several of the old drugs. We could knock the virus down so it's no longer measurable, and if the patient could tolerate the drugs we could keep it down for two to three years. That's where we are today. Even though it's not gone, we can control it. Not in everyone, but in many, many patients, and this result is reflected in the national statistics.

How have the statistics changed?

If one looks at the inpatient census for AIDS patients, it's gone way down. These complicated infections that we call opportunistic infections have gone way down. Most importantly, AIDS mortality has gone down about 50 percent in each of the last two years [1997 and 1998.] Lots of patients have turned around from a very sick state to a functional state where they are able to return to their jobs. . . .

Do you still use AZT in the anti-AIDS cocktail, or has it been replaced?

There are now many different cocktails. We have about twelve drugs against HIV in our armamentarium, and with that you can mix many different combinations. Typically they involve one or two of the protease inhibitors together with several of the older drugs, such as AZT, D14, 3TC. The whole field is trying to learn what the best combinations are. We don't have the final answer, but we know some good combinations.

What is the likelihood that we will see a cure or a vaccine for AIDS in the near future? Do you have any kind of time line in your mind?

Those are our objectives. We want to push the therapy from controlling the virus to curing the virus. We are facing several major obstacles. We know now, having controlled the virus for three years, that in a lot of patients there's still a residual pool of virus, and we have to come up with strategies to flush that out. We have to tickle those viruses out of quiescence so they can be attacked by the drugs that we administer. That's going for the cure, but I can't give you any time line. A vaccine is another goal. These therapeutic advances of the past few years are great for American and European patients who can afford it.

How expensive is this treatment?

The drugs cost about $15,000 a year. You add on all of the testing and the doctor's fee and the hospital and clinic fees, and it's an enormous cost, which is simply out of the question for the patients in other countries. And that's where the epidemic is, numerically speaking. Over 90 percent of AIDS cases occur in Africa, Asia and in developing countries. We're not going to make an impact on the global epidemic of HIV infection through these drugs, so we have to do it through prevention. Prevention can be tackled through education, but as scientists our responsibility is to develop a vaccine. That has been the most difficult task. If HIV were as easy as polio or Hepatitis B or measles, we would have had a vaccine sometime in the mid to late '80s, but it's a different virus. It changes very quickly. It has this shield . . . , and the immune system doesn't see it very well. We need new strategies to come up with a vaccine, so there isn't one now. Even if there was one today, it would take several years to test it and apply it, so a vaccine is still years away. But everyone working in the field realizes . . . how important it is. It's center stage in AIDS research. . . .

How did your association with the Aaron Diamond Center begin?

The Aaron Diamond AIDS Research Center was put together by people in New York. The philanthropist Irene Diamond provided the funds to get it going, and the institute is named for her husband. Some of the city officials as well as Irene Diamond's advisors came up with the idea of concentrating their money and effort on an institute that would be devoted to AIDS research. I agreed with the idea and was recruited to direct the Center. I really appreciate the fact that I was given that opportunity.

Opportunities in America

Do you believe you had opportunities in America that you would not have had somewhere else?

I've lived the American dream so far. Only in America would a 37-year-old be given that opportunity to become an institute director.

I think the culture overall here is enlightened enough to be able to give responsibility to a young person without that much regard for age, and with greater emphasis on merit, on potential, and such things. It's in many ways an amazing experience. I've done well. I was working hard. I had a certain vision of what I wanted to do, and those things fitted well with the goals of the new institute. So I was given the chance and I believe I've taken advantage of that golden opportunity.

I had the same conversation with John Shalikashvili. Only in America would a foreign born person be made Chairman of the Joint Chiefs of Staff as he was, or Secretary of State like Madeleine Albright, who's also foreign born. I think it's fantastic. This would not happen in China, Taiwan, Japan or many of the European countries. I'm truly grateful to be here, and to my father in particular for putting in that tremendous effort during those early, difficult years. This is a very enlightened country.

1830s

Chinese laborers arrive in Hawaii to work in the sugarcane fields; Chinese seamen arrive in New York City.

1849

Gold is discovered in California; Chinese immigrants arrive to seek their fortune in the goldfields.

1850

The Chinese population in America is four thousand out of 23.2 million.

1851

Chinese immigrants form district mutual protection and self-help associations in San Francisco.

1852

California enacts the Foreign Miners' Tax, and the state charges Chinese miners a monthly tax until 1870, when the law is voided by an amendment to the U.S. Constitution.

1865

The Central Pacific Railroad begins recruiting Chinese laborers to build railroads.

1868

China and the United States sign the Burlingame Treaty, which sets out reciprocal rights between the two nations, including the right to immigrate.

1869

Chinese laborers finish the western section of the transcontinental railroad.

1878

The U.S. Supreme Court declares Chinese ineligible to become naturalized American citizens.

1880

San Francisco Chinese district associations form the Chinese Consolidated Benevolent Association (Chung Wah Kung Saw), also known as the Six Companies, to assist and provide emergency aid for Chinese residents of San Francisco.

1882

The U.S. Congress passes the Chinese Exclusion Act, prohibiting immigration of Chinese laborers for ten years; exempted from the act are teachers, diplomats, students, merchants, and travelers; Chinese are not allowed to become naturalized U.S. citizens.

1885

Twenty-eight Chinese miners are massacred at Rock Springs, Wyoming, and an additional fifteen are wounded, some of whom die later; Chinese property is destroyed.

1888

The Scott Act is passed, prohibiting the return of Chinese laborers who left the United States temporarily to visit China.

1892

The Geary Act extends the Chinese Exclusion Act of 1882 for ten additional years.

1898

The U.S. Supreme Court rules that ethnic Chinese children born in the United States are American citizens.

1904

Exclusion of Chinese laborers under the Chinese Exclusion Act of 1882 is extended indefinitely.

1905

Sun Yat-sen organizes the Revolutionary Alliance in Japan with the aim of overthrowing the Qing dynasty in China.

1906

Destruction of records caused by a massive earthquake in San Francisco enables Chinese residents of the city to claim that they are American-born citizens.

1909

An immigration station is established at Angel Island in San Francisco Bay to investigate Chinese immigrants claiming to be related to Chinese American citizens.

1911

Revolutionaries in Wuhan, China, rise up against the Qing dynasty, triggering revolts all over China and initiating the revolution of 1911.

1912

Emperor Pu Yi abdicates the Qing throne, the Republic of China is founded, and Sun Yat-sen becomes provisional president.

1913

California enacts the Alien Land Law, which prevents Chinese and other Asian immigrants and their children from owning land; similar laws are enacted in several other states.

1922

The Cable Act is passed stipulating that any American woman who marries an immigrant who is ineligible to become a citizen—for example, a Chinese man—will lose her U.S. citizenship.

1924

The Immigration Act of 1924 is passed, stipulating that no Chinese woman may enter the United States for the purpose of becoming a permanent resident; children are also denied entry; one year later the Supreme Court permits one exception, merchant wives.

1937

Japan invades China.

1941

Japan attacks the United States; the United States enters World War II as an ally of China.

1943

The Chinese Exclusion Act of 1882 is repealed; a yearly quota of 105 Chinese immigrants is set; this compares to a yearly quota of sixty thousand English immigrants.

1945

America enters World War II; the War Brides Act is passed, stipulating that wives of U.S. servicemen can enter the United States. Approximately six thousand Chinese women enter under this act.

1947–1949

Civil war breaks out in China; the Communists emerge victorious, and Nationalist leader Chiang Kai-shek and his followers flee to Taiwan.

1948

The Displaced Persons Act is passed, giving permanent resident status to Chinese seamen, students, and visitors who fear returning to China because of Communist control.

1949

The People's Republic of China is established and China becomes a Communist state led by Mao Zedong.

1953

The Refugee Relief Act is passed, allowing 2,777 refugees from China to enter the United States.

1962

A presidential directive allows several thousand Chinese immigrants from Hong Kong to enter the United States.

1965

The Immigration Act of October 3, 1965, is passed, abolishing the quota system based on national origin; new quotas are enacted of up to twenty thousand persons each year for each independent country outside the Western Hemisphere; family reunification is now an important goal of immigration.

1981

Taiwan is considered separate from the People's Republic of China and receives a quota of twenty thousand immigrants to the United States.

1986

The Immigration Act of 1986 is passed, increasing the quota for persons born in Hong Kong to five thousand.

1990

The Immigration Act of 1990 is passed. The U.S. census reports that of 248,709,873 Americans, 1,645,472 are ethnic Chinese. Two-thirds of these are first-generation immigrants.

1999

Wen Ho Lee, a U.S. citizen working in the Los Alamos Nuclear Laboratory, is arrested and charged with spying for China. After 278 days in solitary confinement, he is released due to lack of evidence, and the court apologizes to Wen.

2000

The Chinese American population reaches 2,879,636 out of a total U.S. population of 281,421,904.

FOR FURTHER RESEARCH

General Histories

Iris Chang, *The Chinese in America*. New York: Viking, 2003.

Jack Chen, *The Chinese of America*. San Francisco: Harper & Row, 1980.

Gloria Heyung Chun, *Of Orphans and Warriors: Inventing Chinese American Culture and Identity*. New Brunswick, NJ: Rutgers University Press, 2000.

Dorothy Hoobler and Thomas Hoobler, *The Chinese American Family Album*. New York: Oxford University Press, 1994.

Huping Ling, *Surviving on the Gold Mountain: A History of Chinese American Women and Their Lives*. Albany: State University of New York Press, 1998.

Stanford M. Lyman, *Chinese Americans*. New York: Random House, 1974.

Ruthanne Lum McCunn, *Chinese American Portraits: Personal Histories, 1928–1988*. Seattle: University of Washington Press, 1988.

Ronald Takaki, *Strangers from a Different Shore: A History of Asian Americans*. Boston: Little, Brown, 1998.

Benson Tong, *The Chinese Americans*. Westport, CT: Greenwood, 2000.

Shih-Shan Henry Tsai, *The Chinese Experience in America*. Bloomington: Indiana University Press, 1986.

Judy Yung, *Unbound Feet: A Social History of Chinese*

Women in San Francisco. Berkeley and Los Angeles: University of California Press, 1995.

Exclusion Era: 1882–1943

Sucheng Chan, ed., *Entry Denied: Exclusion and the Chinese Community in America, 1882–1943*. Philadelphia: Temple University Press, 1991.

Shehong Chen, *Being Chinese, Becoming Chinese American*. Urbana: University of Illinois Press, 2002.

Andrew Gyory, *Closing the Gate: Race, Politics, and the Chinese Exclusion Act*. Chapel Hill: University of North Carolina Press, 1998.

Him Mark Lai, Genny Lim, and Judy Yung, *Island: Poetry and History of Chinese Immigrants on Angel Island, 1910–1940*. San Francisco: HOC DOI Project of the Chinese Culture Foundation of San Francisco, 1986.

Erika Lee, *At America's Gates: Chinese Immigration During the Exclusion Era, 1882–1943*. Chapel Hill: University of North Carolina Press, 2000.

Ruthanne Lum McCunn, *Thousand Pieces of Gold*. Boston: Beacon, 1981.

World War II to the Present

Ko-Lin Chin, *Smuggled Chinese: Clandestine Immigration to the United States*. Philadelphia: Temple University Press, 1999.

Gwen Kinkead, *Chinatown: Portrait of a Closed Society*. New York: HarperCollins, 1992.

Peter Kwong, *Forbidden Workers: Illegal Chinese Immigrants and American Labor*. New York: New Press, 1997.

———, *The New Chinatown*. New York: Hill and Wang, 1996.

Jan Lin, *Reconstructing Chinatown: Ethnic Enclave,*

Global Change. Minneapolis: University of Minnesota Press, 1998.

Charles J. McClain, ed., *Chinese Immigrants and American Law*. New York: Garland, 1994.

Joan Morrison and Charlotte Fox Zabusky, eds., *American Mosaic: The Immigrant Experience in the World of Those Who Lived It*. New York: Dutton, 1980.

Xiaojian Zhao, *Remaking Chinese America: Immigration, Family, and Community, 1940–1965*. New Brunswick, NJ: Rutgers University Press, 2002.

Essays, Memoirs, and Family Histories

May-Lee Chai and Winberg Chai, *The Girl from Purple Mountain*. New York: St. Martin's, 2001.

Pang-Mei Natasha Chang, *Bound Feet and Western Dress*. New York: Doubleday, 1996.

Tung Pok Chin, with Winifred C. Chin, *Paper Son: One Man's Story*. Philadelphia: Temple University Press, 2000.

Ben Fong-Torres, *The Rice Room: Growing Up Chinese-American—from Number Two Son to Rock 'n' Roll*. New York: Hyperion, 1994.

Bruce Edward Hall, *Tea That Burns: A Family Memoir of Chinatown*. New York: Free Press, 1998.

Hamilton Holt, ed., *The Life Stories of (Undistinguished) Americans*. New York: Routledge, 1990.

Maxine Hong Kingston, *China Men*. New York: Knopf, 1980.

———, *The Woman Warrior: Memoirs of a Girlhood Among Ghosts*. New York: Knopf, 1977.

Michelle Kwan, as told to Laura James, *Michelle Kwan, Heart of a Champion: An Autobiography*. New York: Scholastic, 1997.

Gus Lee, *Chasing Hepburn: A Memoir of Shanghai, Hollywood, and a Chinese Family's Fight for Freedom.* New York: Harmony Books, 2002.

Eric Liu, *The Accidental Asian: Notes of a Native Speaker.* New York: Random House, 1998.

M. Elaine Mar, *Paper Daughter: A Memoir.* New York: HarperCollins, 1999.

Lisa See, *On Gold Mountain.* New York: St. Martin's, 1991.

Jade Snow Wong, *Fifth Chinese Daughter.* Seattle: University of Washington Press, 1989.

Laurence Yep, *The Lost Garden.* Englewood Cliffs, NJ: Messner, 1991.

Web Sites

Angel Island: Immigrant Journeys of Chinese Americans, www.angel-island.com/history.html. This site provides historical information, photos, and interviews with former detainees who passed through Angel Island.

Becoming American: The Chinese Experience, www.pbs. org/becomingamerican/chineseexperience.html. The PBS television series on Chinese Americans includes histocial review of the Chinese in America and interviews with prominent Chinese Americans.

Chinese Historical Society of America, www.chsa.org. Events and exhibits at the Chinese Historical Society's museum in San Francisco are found at this site.

Immigration Station, Angel Island, www.angelisland. org/immigr02. html. Maps, photos, and historical commentary on the Angel Island center are included.

Museum of Chinese in the Americas, www.moca-nyc.org/ MoCA/content.asp. Events and exhibits at the Museum of Chinese in the Americas in New York City are included.

INDEX